The All of the All

LAURA SALTMAN

SAVAAH
MEDIA

The All of the All
The All of Everything, Book 2

DISCLAIMER

The information and opinions expressed here are believed to be accurate based on the best judgement available to the author. This book is intended to be educational, as a means to guide you on your spiritual journey. The author of this book does not dispense medical advice or prescribe the use of any technique as a form of treatment for physical, emotional or medical problems without the advice of a physician or medical professional. In the event you use any of the information in this book for yourself, the author and the publisher assume no responsibility for your actions.

Cover by Wendy Kis

Back cover photo by Liz Kane & Co.

The book is dedicated to
all of us willingly searching for answers
to the great mysteries of life.

Introduction

When I wrote my first book, *The All of Everything*, I had no idea what sort of journey was in store for me. I never imagined something so starkly informative would come out of my mind and be written through my fingertips. I simply sat down and began typing questions for the Universe into my laptop in the middle of the night and started receiving answers instantaneously; I certainly wasn't planning on writing a book, nor did I know I would be capable of delivering 400-plus pages of spiritual guidance and wisdom in just a few months. The feat was nothing short of a miracle, which is why I knew the material needed to be shared. The way the book and the revelations therein had come about was so mind boggling, so otherworldly, so beyond my own personal ability or intellect that I decided they had to be published regardless of my reservations and fear.

The whole process began in July 2017 when I was going through a particularly rough patch in my life. Though I had my son, who is my biggest blessing, the rest of the circumstances of my life were a wreck. My brother had died from stomach cancer in late 2013, and my distraught father committed suicide shortly thereafter. I had struggled through infertility, I had suffered two miscarriages, and I was heartbroken after three failed adoption attempts (the last of which was on the day the baby was born) which led to my marriage crumbling. I had also walked away from my career as an entertainment reporter; it had been in turmoil after my attempts to advance further as a host in the industry were thwarted time after time. My beloved dogs Raven and Paris had also passed away. This nonstop barrage of tragic circumstances had taken its toll on my health, both mentally and physically. I needed a break from life.

I had decided to move from Los Angeles to Florida to take that break and be closer to my remaining family. I struggled to find myself and gain my footing even with the help of a spiritual life coach guiding me on my journey. She did, however, help me unlock an intuitive gift I had known about since my early twenties—clairaudience. I had the ability to clearly hear those in spirit in my mind and become a channel.

It was through the process of opening up to spirituality that I found myself able to use my journalism background to listen and create a conversation, an interview really, with what most people would term "God." Some call it Spirit, Source, the Universe, or Divine Mind. I called it God—not because that is where my beliefs fell but because that was how I received it as I wrote. I was told during my channeling to purposefully present it this "God" way, much like how Neale Donald Walsch did in *Conversations with God*,[1] because it would appeal to a larger audience and help those seeking enlightenment. That material became my book *The All of Everything: A Spiritual Guide to Inner World Domination*.

From writing *The All of Everything*, I now understand that we are all just energy. There is only one energy, one Source, one giant being of light and love split into infinite parts; each of us has individual consciousness, but we are also part of a collective consciousness and the Oneness. Anytime we are in a higher state of *being* and *knowing*, we return to Oneness. Our minds are joined again, and this is when we are capable of talking to God, Source, or the Universe through our inner being because there is only one of us here—a single Divine Mind split into trillions upon trillions of parts in various shapes and forms within a vast cosmos.

As I wrote, I grappled with fears, doubts, and worries, and I used those as fuel for my questions. Over the course of those few months, God, or Spirit, described in stark detail how we are the creators of our circumstances through our thoughts, words, and actions; through my inner voice I was reminded of who we truly are at the core—divine beings of light and love here to grow and evolve our souls.

The information provided in the pages of *The All of Everything* was life altering for me and yet so simple and easy to understand. We are never alone. We are always guided by an unseen force, which lives inside of us and waits to be awakened. However, putting the ideas presented in that book into practice in my life was where I got hung up. My life wasn't exactly working the way the book told me it could. I realize now that was because I wasn't being consistent in my spiritual practices. I was still skeptical. So when I finished that book, I had many, many more questions. While I prepared the first book for publishing, I continued our nightly Q&A sessions. In fact, I was told there would be three books written in this *All* series and that each book's name would be given to me during our conversations. I came to understand that these highs and lows of my life were quite purposeful for the creation of these books. My mess was creating the perfect message for others to benefit. In order to create the books, I had to be guided into certain feelings and circumstances through my own soul.

If I thought the last book was incredible and insightful, this second book is even more miraculous with information, advice, and ideas that exceed anything I could have ever imagined or dreamed up. It is remarkable in its own way and significantly different from the first book in that it details our connection to the cosmos and not just the universe. We are part of not only one universe, but also an immense multiplex of universes all split off from the Oneness. Quantum physicists, scientists, astronomers, and astronauts are among the many people who are beginning to understand this cosmic truth and work toward proving it.

As you read this book, know that I don't identify with any religious background, and I have not done any specific religious research; this means that what you read here is directly from "the source" with no outside religious influence. I made no edits to the concepts discussed. I simply asked a question and was given an answer from the quiet voice within my mind. There was no lag time between the question and the answer—I heard the answers instantaneously as if I was having a conversation with someone. I like to call it an inner dictation. I typed as the voice talked.

I will admit some of the conversations I share here shocked me to my core, but just as I did in my last book, I share them here because I wrote something so monumentally different from how I personally think and believe that I knew it had to be a truth. Some of the medical concepts I write about, especially those dealing with autism, allergies, and other illnesses, are immensely radical. As much as I wanted to remove them from the book, I couldn't bring myself to delete them. It was as if my fingers refused too. Spirit describes in stark detail how humanity manifests illnesses and offers ways to work toward healing them; knowing how this book came to be written, I fully believe we can.

I share this book not to alarm but to inform. I share this book to help as many people as I can wake up to the truths of the universe. I could not save my brother from his terminal cancer diagnosis, and I could not save my dad from taking his own life. But if I can help even just a few people remember who they truly are so that they may begin to consciously create in their own lives and break the cycle of depression, anger, resentment, and illness, then I will have honored my brother's and dad's memory and accomplished my soul's true purpose. It took me forty-six years to learn my purpose and to finally understand the meanings and reasons behind so many of my decisions in life.

May you also find your purpose within these pages.

Always Be Willing

" *D ear God, Universe, Source, as we cocreate this second book, may we share any and all universal truths with all who have come seeking and wish to know themselves from a standpoint of mind-body-soul. Together we shall remove any and all words that come from an ego mind. Amen.*"

Laura: What is the greatest thing I can do for myself today, something we all can do every day of our lives to bring us happiness?

God: Be present. Be available to witness the magic that all of life has to offer. As long as you are staying present, you are noticing and witnessing the miracles of creation. You are never without your go-to team, which is all of us together. We are with you always and forever.

L: Thank you as always for your wisdom and guidance. Something happened to me today that I felt was a sign for me. I found a small little bird—

G: A sparrow.

L: Yes, a beautiful sparrow who had died on my back porch. He (or she) must have flown accidentally into my sliding glass door.

G: Perhaps. Or perhaps nothing tragic befell this little bird, but rather, it was a message of hope and inspiration for you.

L: A dead bird on my porch is hopeful?

G: In most cases, if not all, animals are miracle messengers. They bring tidings of love and transformation for all who stumble upon them. Your bird was perhaps a tiny little messenger telling you that life as you know it is about to change for the better. Your world is changing. You are taking flight and ready to fly to massive heights. You did pray for this answer and for that little bird's soul, did you not?

L: I did.

G: And we will answer you always. Forever are we here.

L: What about the dream last night I had about an alligator in the water? I had to swim away before it chased me. Or at least, I felt as if it were going to chase me. Will you please reveal the true nature of this dream to me?

G: Here may we congratulate you on a job well done. For your readers, we will note that it was not until you asked for the answer, prayed for it, that we were able to bring this to you. You paused for a moment and heard nothing at all. Then you went back and wrote your prayer (asking), and in that asking we may now reveal the answer. The alligator is a harbinger of doom— irrational thoughts below the surface. Where are you holding on to fear, one may ask, when such a dream occurs.

L: Where am I holding on to fear?

G: Your fears are many. Fears of doubt are rampant. How shall I sell my book (your last book we cowrote)? Where shall I live next? How shall I survive when I have no money coming in from a steady job? What mark is this on my arm? Is this the mark of cancer? Who will love me? How may I learn to love myself? What's my destiny when it comes to more children? What may come my way? Does this not sound familiar, resonate within one's soul?

L: It sure does. I feel so blessed to have written our first book, but if I am being honest, yes, I am terrified about all those things above. So how do—well, no, I know how now. What would be the proper prayer to release all these irrational thoughts and fears?

G: First, we may say to go to see a doctor if you are unclear on any medical issue. We wish to say here that as the All of Everything, you are not impervious to illness, as irrational thoughts may be deeply rooted within your subconscious. For one may not know what lies beneath the surface both literally and figuratively. So a plan for peace shall be attempted moment by moment, day by day, until all irrational thoughts are released. Until that time, take the medicine. See the doctor. Explore the subconscious mind's irrational thoughts as a means of clearing blocks to salvation. Repeat prayers, but also reclaim your health through practical medicine. One day, all who come to know God will have no need for medicines.

L: I am not sure this is making me feel better. Actually, this is making me feel more fear, as if you are issuing a warning.

G: My dear, you asked for an explanation of your dream state, and here we are providing this to you. It is upon you not to interpret it as a death sentence or a declaration of illness. We are merely pointing out that unless and until you have cleared all mental and spiritual blocks to health, a diagnosis is practical. This does not mean the diagnosis is imminent, nor does it mean it is not. We are simply saying that all who hide hidden fears must organize their thinking until the issues are resolved. This means, as we have stated above, take the pill, seek the medicine, and ask the doctor, but also clear the mind from a spiritual standpoint. Doing these in conjunction with each other will have a marked improvement over the typical human modality of going on the internet and allowing a device to decide for you. Dr. Google or Dr. God? You decide.

L: I will take Dr. God.

G: A wise choice, indeed.

L: So I will make an appointment with my doctor, but let's write that prayer too.

G: "Dear God, remove from my mind any and all irrational thoughts keeping me stuck in cyclical patterns of destructive self-abuse and condemnation. Allow my true nature to shine through, as I know I am a child of the All of Everything, and the spirit within holds all truth of this. Together may we think a new thought, see a whole healthy body. Amen."

L: But even when I do say those prayers, eventually new thoughts arise. You have said that in any instant our irrational thoughts are healed when we return them to Spirit/God/ Universe, etc. So which is it?

G: Think an instant. Stay an instant. In order to stay in transformation, one must do exactly that—stay in transformation. This is why we say in any "instant" may you return unhealed thoughts to the maker. This is not to say that once you have a healed thought it will always stay so. Reminding all who come seeking this re-information that you are all at choice of which thoughts to think in each and every moment of your current circumstances. Rarely do those at prayer stay in prayer; irrationally do they return to the irrational process of thought, which guards an ego mind. This is the importance of stillness, quietude, or meditation, as it releases repetitive thought patterns, such as "I am not good enough. I don't believe in all of this nonsense of universal principles."

Practice makes perfect, and in each and every moment may one pray for a new result, such as "Release this pattern of thought so that we may be healed. Amen."

L: I feel as if it is somewhat impossible to stay consistent with this. I wish we had a light switch so we could shut the irrational thoughts down, because the truth is that keeping your thoughts in a space of peace, love, and joy can sometimes feel impossible. At the end of the day we are surrounded by naysayers and negativity, be it from our own family and friends or things we see posted on the internet or on social media. It's just nonstop negativity. If there were a secret

formula for releasing these irrational thoughts permanently, I would love to know about it, because frankly, I am sick and tired of feeling these ups and downs and highs and lows that I know are prevalent with others who would be reading these books and materials.

G: Think an instant. Stay an instant. We shall remind you again, as we have above, that those in transformation only stay in transformation by right-minded rational thinking. There is no magic sauce or secret formula to this other than to say you are at the mercy of your will.

L: Can you explain that further please, being at the mercy of our will?

G: Your will is the road map, the designer of your life. It is the deepest most subconscious parts of who you are at the core— which is pure spirit. Set forth by you, for you, was a grander vision of who and what you really are. From a standpoint of mind-body-soul, you asked the creative power within you to design a life whereby you could undo all learned behaviors from any and all subsequent and simultaneous lifetimes, thereby eradicating the need for them in other incarnations. To be at the mercy of your will is to remind yourself of these sacred contracts (a truth we will discuss in further detail later in this material), which are very much at play in all lifetimes simultaneously. You cannot escape all circumstances. The simple fact that you are here to learn, grow, and evolve makes it impossible to remove some of these persistent and consistent memories, which are causing you to feel as if life is randomly happening to you and not through you. We can, however, very much tell you that you are the designer and decorator of your life's circumstances. You bring scenarios and situations to you through the power of your thoughts, words, and actions. Your will is our will, and so whenever thoughts align back to the Oneness, why, then you may cocreate a new circumstance in which you may move through any and all chosen scenarios from which to grow and evolve much, much quicker.

L: I still don't feel as if you are explaining how we are at the mercy of our will here.

G: Your will is our will. Your want is our want. Your ask is our ask. You will get what you both want and don't want through the power of your thoughts, words, and actions.

L: But isn't my will always for happy, positive things? Why would I will things that I don't want to happen?

G: Because you may not know what you are willing. You may want and need something, but your will may be opposite of these things.

L: Can you give me an example please?

G: We may. You want a baby. You need money. You desire a result whereby when the money comes, the baby will come. Your will is to connect with a part of you that feels missing. All three (want/ need/desire) are attainable whenever thoughts align back to the Oneness.

L: OK, but that is an example of something where all things are in cahoots. Now will you give me an example where the will clashes with the wants and needs?

G: We may. However, we will point out that you did not ask

us this question initially. We are mind readers, and yet we are not. You must be clear and specific on what you want, need, and desire in order for the energy within to manifest that which you all truly are. Ask your question again, and be mindful that it is clear and specific please.

L: Will you please present an example of when our will clashes with our wants and needs?

G: We may. Now we shall give you a clear and specific example based on your clear and specific question. You want this book to be a success. You need followers and/or people to read your book. You will not let go of your fears, doubts, and worries.

L: I don't want to keep doing that. I am willing to let go of my need to control everything.

G: Have you shown this in your actions and reactions as it relates to money and the release of these books and materials?

L: No. I keep repeating the same thought patterns over again.

G: Be willing to see it differently, and you will. Your will is our will. Your ask is our ask, but you are at the mercy of your will and your ego. Together they are the perfect storm of misbegotten energy and misguided guidance.

L: I try. I really try. I get there, and then I return back to the fear. I am willing to let go of my need to control everything. I am willing to practice more of what you preach. I am willing to see things differently. I am willing to let go of my past and live in the present moment.

G: For this is all you truly have. Only the present moment is what counts in your current lifetime or incarnation. Be present. Be willing. Always be willing so your will may be our will.

L: But if my will is for change deep down, then what am I doing wrong here?

G: From a standpoint of right and wrong as we see things, nothing. From a standpoint of being willing, you are not. You are, in fact, willing yourself not to be what it is you say you wish to be by the sheer knowledge that you are currently not what you say you wish to be. Therefore, you are willing yourself not to be. Your will is our will, but only in the absence of fear is when that which you are willing yourself to be may appear. Make sense?

L: I think I am just super confused by this whole conversation about our "will." Can you describe for me in clear and concise language the definition from a spiritual level as to what our "will" actually is?

G: A will in the realm of the physical is an agreement between two or more parties that states, "These are my wishes after I have left the earthly (or otherworldly) plane. You may distribute my wealth, income, and belongings among all named party members in the agreement."

What would happen if, say, the parties did not agree upon the terms of the agreement and fought to have it contested?

L: Then they would go to court and fight it I guess?

G: And what would happen to the will?

L: It would sit idly until either the parties came to an agreement or a judge declared the will uncontestable or unenforceable.

G: In the realm of the spiritual, your will works in much the same way. Your agreements in the physical world are set forth by you, for you. Consider yourself both the testator and the contester. You (the testator) may say your will is for change, but your ego (the contester) does not agree with your will and will, therefore, do everything in its power to contest this action until you (the judge, in this case) decide for yourself (the testator) what is best for all parties involved (i.e., you and your ego).

L: I think that makes sense. Explanations like that really make it clear that I am not writing this book as just Laura. How in the world I could have come up with something like that in ten seconds is beyond my present capabilities as a journalist. That would have required a lot of research on my part. So we set forth our wills, but whenever our ego is around, it holds us hostage so we can't actually get to what it is we say our will is to be, do, or have?

G: Precisely. Very good. You are understanding more now?

L: Yes. I think so.

G: We may discuss this further later on as well; if you are willing.

L: Very funny.

G: We are funny.

Doctor's Orders

" **D**ear God and All of the Universe, here now may we discover radical truths about our very nature of being. Amen."

Laura: I went to the doctor this week, and sure enough, I had an issue when it came to my arm. It wasn't cancer fortunately, but it was an atypical mole, which had to be removed surgically. Let me get this straight here. You are saying that I was the creator of that circumstance?

God: Yes. Irrational thoughts below the surface (as we had inscribed here earlier). Circumstances surrounding the All of Everything are always at play whenever ego has you caught in its clutches. The mark on your arm is a direct reflection of your innermost demons of irritability in relation to aging. Your focused attention upon it is what brought it to the surface both literally and figuratively. Has the issue not been resolved to your liking?

L: It has.

G: And why do you think that is?

L: **It is because I prayed over it; I made my peace with it. I understood its meaning and acted in a manner consistent with what is being taught here by you through me.**

G: A job well done, indeed. There is no irrationally created manifestation of illness that cannot be healed through focused intention and prayerful modalities.

L: **But people who pray, set intentions, and understand our connection to the All That Is still die from illnesses all the time. So it's not always a cure all.**

G: No, but as we have said prior, there is no *irrationally* created manifestation of illness that cannot be healed through these methods. There is, however, at play a purposeful role for illnesses for those who are ready to leave the earthly plane behind. Once one has incarnated, they have a choice always for the thoughts, words, and actions of their lives. One may choose to leave any way they decide upon once the soul is ready to return.

L: **Well, then what's the use of praying and using all these spiritual tools if we have no choice in the matter and the soul is in charge?**

G: Because you are at choice in the matter when you are "of body" and one may not know the soul's "plan of attack," so to speak. So one may always turn to God or Spirit as a means to heal, but yes, at some point there will be souls who are returning righteously by choice.

L: But just in case our illness is caused by irrational or subconscious thinking, we should always use our spiritual tools to try to heal it?

G: Yes. We remind you here as well that you have a choice in the matter always as both body and mind and, therefore, should always turn to God or Spirit for accurate presentation of what is truth and what is illusion.

L: Does our soul ever choose to get sick? Do we cause illness we decide upon prior to incarnating?

G: Yes, and we will give you an example a little bit later in this dialogue.

L: What about a child who gets sick? Right now, it is the middle of the night, and my son is struggling to breathe from some upper respiratory issue yet again. How may I help him since children often don't use prayer when asked even if they are taught to?

G: Children, from the standpoint of God or the All of Everything, are perfectly capable, as are adults, of releasing irrational thought leading to illness. It is not upon a parent to remind them of their true nature (as they are too young yet to understand this truly); rather, it is upon a parent to release children from the grips of over protection.

L: So on some level, parents are at cause for a child getting sick?

G: For this is not what we are saying at all. We are merely saying irrational minds perpetuate all illness by believing that whatever is happening to them, or to a child, is truly happening rather than believing it to be of an illusional nature. Which is more accurate: "My child is sick" or "My child thinks he is sick and is, therefore, manifesting reactionary ailments to inner subconscious thoughts"?

L: Subconscious thoughts are causing the issue at hand?

G: If one knows this, what may one say to alleviate and reduce the time frame of the illness?

L: I don't know the proper words. Will you please inscribe them here with me now?

G: And we are glad you asked.

"Father of all children, here now may we cocreate an experience with my child where whatever illness they believe to be suffering is removed from their subconscious mind. Together may we hold space for their perfect healing through both spiritual and science-based modalities. As we undertake this, shall they be healed and reminded of their true nature through subconscious means of prayer and intention practiced by parents and loved ones around them. Amen."

L: Are you saying that children are not capable of healing themselves?

G: We are saying children need subconscious-level attention through focused prayer. They alone are not capable at this point in their earthly evolutions to enact the change needed for instantaneous or spontaneous healing.

L: So when a child is sick, it is upon us to say what to them to help them heal?

G: "My dear, you are feeling well. You will be up and out of bed in no time. You have no need to worry, my child. You are being well taken care of. Mommy and Daddy (or Daddy and Daddy, Mommy and Mommy, Aunty, Grandma)—"

L: I get the point.

G: We knew you would.

"Please remember Mommy and I love you and are here to make you feel better. Soon you will be back on the playground, and in no time you will be feeling back to normal."

L: Reassurance?

G: Subconscious reminders.

L: How is that subconscious?

G: The deeper parts of their minds are reachable by way of intentional prayer. One needs never to panic when a child takes ill but rather remind themselves of the illusional-based nature of illness. Simply administer the medicine, but never consciously break from the notion that a child's illness is any more real than your own.

L: But children don't know this, so how can we help them more immediately? Like right now, my son is struggling to breathe, and it's breaking my heart.

G: He is sleeping soundly, no?

L: Yes.

G: A perfect time to infuse his subconscious mind. Walk over to him now, stroke his hair, and say, "My dear one, release the thoughts that are leading to this persistent childhood affliction of colds, coughs, and breathing problems. In your sleep may you dream of a healthier tomorrow so when you awaken you are healed. Amen."

L: I love that, but what happens if they wake up still sick?

G: Simply state, "You are feeling better. I knew you would. Just wait until tomorrow; you will be back to normal."

L: And what should we not be saying or doing?

G: "Oh no!" Frantic running around or panicked movements are not helpful but rather harmful to children. For in your panic are they frazzled too.

L: Well, I failed that test tonight. I panicked.

G: And so we shall begin again.

L: We shall. OK, I am going to try it your way.

I walked over to my son, put my hand on his forehead, and said the subconscious prayer to him.

G: You said it, and how did it make you feel?

L: Hopeful.

G: Miracles abound whenever one remind themselves of their true nature. A child, in this way, may be reminded as well.

L: So is this what you meant by subconsciously talking to them in their sleep?

G: Talk to them in their sleep and in their waking moments. Children are susceptible to our collective parental thoughts in both cases. We must, however, keep thoughts bound to a right-minded nature.

"You are well," not "You are sick." "You will feel better as soon as possible," not "I'm sorry you are sick." "You are brave," not "You are weak." "You are strong and will get through this quickly," not "I hope you don't have to miss too many days of school for this."

L: I am glad you brought this up. Why do kids get sick constantly? My son is excited to miss school. Is this perhaps how kids' irrational thoughts affect their bodies through their minds?

G: All thoughts are reactive. Kids bring about illness through the power of their thoughts just as adults do. Teachers, other students, parents, and school nurses all create an environment where these repetitive illnesses are possible. No child need suffer endlessly from repetitive colds. Undertaking the modalities we have inscribed here with you shall help alleviate many of these occurrences.

L: But not all of them?

G: No, for upon your society lies the plague of mankind, which states that children must undergo certain ailments.

L: What about kids with autism?

G: We had touched on this in our first book, and here may we reveal the truths of childhood illnesses, be they big or small. All minds connected. All minds responsible. Fear begets fear begets fear. No child need suffer from said afflictions in the mind of God. Children are by and by at the mercy of their families' wills until they may cocreate a new circumstance.

L: Wait, wait, wait. You said in our other book that we choose experiences from which we may grow and evolve our soul. Wouldn't that apply to autism and other childhood diseases?

G: A death circumstance at a young age, for the purpose of knowing the idea of long and short, is rightly chosen by one incarnating for said purpose. A childhood illness such as autism, Asperger's syndrome, and types of cancers that are curable, such as Hodgkin lymphoma or leukemia, are illusions based solely upon one's own pattern of thought predominantly made manifest by those around them. A parent, a doctor, a nurse, a friend, another family member, such as a grandparent or aunt/uncle. We have told you that all minds are connected, and therefore, no one thinks a thought that does not have an effect on the collective consciousness of the whole. Therefore, all minds react off one another. Children are susceptible as well.

L: Oh my god. So you are trying to tell me that all these childhood illnesses are all of our faults? No one will buy that. I'm sorry. I just can't accept or believe that a child can be

affected this way. No way. My little cousin had leukemia when she was two and a half years old. I cannot understand that being all of our collective faults.

G: Perhaps one needs to be reminded of the collective nature of consciousness before doubting inner truths. All minds connected. All minds responsible. No one being upon your planet can think a thought without it binding it to all others. This is a law of the universe, which shall not and cannot be broken. It is uncommon law.

L: Uncommon law? What do you mean by that?

G: Uncommon as in a truth, which one finds hard to rectify and justify, as it creates chaos upon all currently suffering within this illusion.

L: Well, absolutely. The autism community and parents of children who are currently sick would be livid and agitated if they read this because we are basically blaming them. Why did I just write "we"?

G: We is you and me, and we *is* them. As difficult as these concepts may be to describe and inscribe (our word we use for writing with "God") for the one who is tasked with revealing them, one cannot not know the truth within. So they may fight the words as they inscribe them, but inscribe them they must, knowing full well within one's soul is truth.

L: Well, then is there a fix, a cure?

G: Yes, put a stop to all ungodly, uncommon, ununiversal notions of separation, and begin again to cocreate with the we within.

L: Lots and lots of people, perhaps millions upon millions, pray to help their children with these issues. Families, friends, and entire communities sometimes pray upon the sick and needy. Yet, kids still are autistic, still have cancer, and still suffer diseases from which they sometimes die.

G: Prayer, as a means to know God, is right and necessary for all. Prayer, however, is not a cure-all modality unless and until all who seek to know God know God—that is to say one must believe fully in the concept of a cocreator, a sideline cheerleader along for the ride all of the all of their lives in order for miracles to occur. A true miracle is not necessary for those knowing inner truths—illnesses are of the mind, not the body. One who truly comprehends this factual truth may be returned to the kingdom of heaven, at once, from a spiritual perspective. This is not to say healing will be instantaneous, as it may take time to release subconscious inner thoughts leading to the root cause of perceived illnesses. However, should one return their thoughts to the maker repetitively and stay there, then shall healing be done unto them.

L: But you just said earlier that because children are not yet ready, they are not capable of healing themselves. First of all, at what age does a kid become ready to tackle universal truths, and second, how does this all work? Do the parents need to be the only ones keeping their thoughts in alignment with God or Source? And also, what about the doctors who are just perpetuating the problem?

G: All problems are of a perpetual nature. See a sickness. Speak a sickness. Create more of the same in others. Don't you know God is behind all so-called illnesses?

L: What do you mean by that?

G: As always, we are glad you asked. All illusion-based thoughts are brought about by wrong-minded (ego) thinking. Therefore, all diagnoses are of God, as all minds bind together as one.

L: Well, then can't God stop this from happening? Doesn't God have free will to say, "Hey, I don't like this doctor's illusion-based diagnosis. Let's cancel this one out so more kids or people don't get this"?

G: God does not pick and choose whom to harm and whom to heal. All minds are bound by their creations, even God's.

L: So God is responsible too for its manifestations?

G: Yes.

L: Really?

G: Yes. Of course, God (as many have deemed to call the system of energy from which we all emanate) is responsible for his or her or its own thoughts. All minds think. I am, therefore, at cause. You asked if God is more powerful than anyone else (in the last book), and I did answer no. You inscribed this and never questioned it. Why do you think that is?

L: Because I knew it would set off a firestorm for the all of humanity, which believes that God is the almighty powerful being.

G: "God" is the almighty powerful being but is also in all of you. Therefore, we are all powerful beings of light and love. The difference, of which you have heard and inscribed prior, is that God (your chosen word here) created and was not created. This is the only difference between you and I and we. God is very much responsible for its own thought patterns as well. No one of us thinks alone. As much as I would enjoy trading attack thoughts in each and every one of my brethren, the law of the universe allows for free will, and therefore, this is simply not spiritually sound or possible to do. God cannot change that which you are not willing to change within your thinking. When God says, "I am behind all illnesses," what I mean by this is that the God within is responsible just as the God without is responsible. All minds create together and, therefore, cannot separate from the whole. We are the sum of all parts, a merry choir of voices shouting loudly or quietly speaking—be it good or bad, sad or happy. A band of brothers and sisters bound throughout eternity and beyond.

L: Though I haven't written it, I notice that whenever you finish a thought, you say amen at the end of the sentence now, which didn't happen in our last book. Why do you do this?

G: So you will know when we are finished with a dialogue and may move on. Shall we move on?

L: I think I need to take a break, think about this for a while, and reread this a few times because its—wait, you did not answer my question about children. How can we remind children who have autism or cancer of their connection to the Universe? At what age is it possible for them to understand the concepts of mind-body-soul and cocreating with the Universe/Source or God?

G: At what age depends on at what stage the child is in development physically, emotionally, and spiritually. One need be reminded of his or her true nature whenever curiosity begins to peak. When questions arise about God or the Universe (dependent upon which term has been taught or used in said one's home environment), then and only then should topics be discussed. Whenever those in choir with children speak of God theology, then they are instilling their own beliefs rather than allowing the child to experience this for itself. One should never undertake a radical notion of explanation of any one path to God using one's own viewpoint.

L: Well, what about someone, like me, who believes fully in the concept of mind-body-soul? I want to teach my child to cocreate with the Universe.

G: Same answer. It is upon all sentient beings of light to prescribe to a concept of creationism so that all who seek to know God (Source/Universe) shall experience this for themselves.

L: But when my son went to the hospital over the summer and we used our minds together and practiced what we are preaching here, I explained to him to pray to God and the Universe to help him.

G: There is nothing wrong, or right, about this approach; we are simply stating it is best to wait until a child is ready. Perhaps your son in this current incarnation is perfectly capable of understanding universal principles. Growth of soul is paramount in attaining inner wisdom, be it child or adult. Whenever one is ready, one will speak to this.

"Mommy (or Daddy or other parental figures), where do babies come from?" or "What makes us who we are?" are starting points for conversation.

Then and only then are children capable of creating circumstances of healing for themselves emotionally and physically, be they six or sixteen or sixty. Some may never be ready though we know most are certainly capable of resonating with universal truths at some point in their earthly (or other worldly) pursuits of soul growth. Casting aside one's ego is the quickest way to salvation, and until one knows and understands oneself from an ego perspective—who am I in relation to other people—only then may one relate.

L: So if a child is an "old soul," they may be ready sooner?

G: Growth of soul is the driving factor here, yes.

L: Well, this makes sense because I know and have been told by you that my son and I have been together through many lifetimes. So he would definitely be an "old soul." I feel bad that I have been pushing this upon him perhaps too early.

G: There is no right or wrong in this evolutionary universe. We are here to present universal truths and remind all of humanity of its true nature. What works for some may not work for others. We are simply showing you a better way. This is not "my way or the highway" but rather "a sharp turn to the left may get us there sooner."

L: Left being LOVE, as we explained in our last book. We either choose the love side of life—left—or the fear side of life—right. Left. Right. You decide, we wrote.

G: Absolute perfection. Are you understanding now?

L: Yes. One last question on this topic. So can a child diagnosed with autism or Asperger's syndrome recover completely in your summation?

G: Beyond all reason and doubt is truth. One who is ready to undertake healing modalities of returning to one's source, in any and all times of need, may create miracles. Once a child is ready, then yes, miraculous healing can and will take place once the child understands the illusionary-based nature of his or her illnesses.

L: But why would a child create a circumstance such as autism for itself?

G: As we have just stated, it is upon those in choir to put a stop to irrational thought patterns leading to radicalized notions of ailments, such as autism and Asperger's syndrome.

L: Well, then let's talk about people who develop something like MS or ALS in their lifetimes. Is this a created circumstance or a chosen experience prior to incarnating?

G: Yes.

L: What do you mean yes? I hate when you do that!

G: Then we will do it more often. What you hate, you create. It is both chosen and created. For all who wish to know themselves must discover for themselves what it means to live within a body whereby they cannot control their functions normally. For some this is chosen prior; for others this is a created circumstance. In either case, healing is readily available. Though one cannot control the length of the stay, one may control the severity if they have chosen for this incarnation a circumstance for this. For one who has created the experience through their thoughts, words, and actions, whenever fear is absent, one may set themselves on a path to healing as long as they stay actively in pursuit of enlightenment.

L: Wow. I just can't wrap my head around this, but then I think why on earth would I write something like this and find myself unable to go back and erase it.

G: Though you can. It is your free will to do so.

L: Can you give me a ballpark sum on how many have created and how many have chosen prior to incarnating?

G: 50/50

L: Seriously?

G: 50/50 is precisely accurate, yes, in relation to all upon the particular planet on which you are currently living.

L: Does this apply to a child born with autism?

G: Absolutely. When a child is ready, it is remedied. We remind all that from a godly perspective, all asks have been answered. Therefore, one's complete and totally healing of said illness has occurred already in the eyes of the Universe. All things exist as possibility. Should one return any and all fear-based thoughts back to the Oneness, to God/the Universe, then shall a healing begin to take hold and begin to manifest as ultimate healing reality.

L: Does that 50/50 rule apply here to autism?

G: No. It is not necessary for one to suffer any mindful afflictions such as these. May we re-mind you of the nature of your being? A mind we will never waste. Bodies are disposable. Minds may be compromised via egoic thinking (both individually and collectively) but cannot and will not be replaced ever; a circumstance such as autism occurs whenever a breakdown of ego has occurred by all minds in choir with one another. We shall reveal here that he who diagnoses it damns it to all others. One's time (of a healing profession) may well better be spent on healing the root cause of all illnesses rather than diagnosing new and noteworthy ones.

L: But children with autism, I would imagine, would have a difficult time because they are slightly or more behind other children. If their minds are impacted because of the illness, how would they get to even being curious about how the Universe works? Wouldn't it be difficult to find a spiritual path for them even if their parents were helping them?

G: It would not be necessary for all those in choir to correct an error in judgement, but rather, it would be beneficial for all (in relation to a child) to spend their time on mindful pursuits of internal awareness.

Upon each parent or guardian have we placed a way to bind awareness.

L: So because our minds can be bound with our children's minds, we can pray for them and help spark a difference?

G: Yes, especially in those with mindful afflictions who cannot yet think for themselves free of the irrational notions of others in choir around them.

L: But how would children like this even get to the point where they are asking the bigger questions about life or God or where we all come from if their minds are affected?

G: How, then, would one in choir with others affect all? This is what you are not yet understanding still. All minds joined as one. A mind is manipulated in choir with another. If you see a monster, why, then you will create upon them the potential for bitterness and hate. If you see a butterfly, why, then you would create upon them a potential for great gratitude and love. See a sickness. Speak a sickness. Spark a sickness. See a joy. Speak a joy. Spark a miracle.

L: So see those children as the miracles they are? OK, now I am crying. I am not sure if it's happy tears or sad tears.

G: It is both happy and sad.

L: Yes, because knowing how our world currently operates, most people will dismiss all of this as silly new age mumbo jumbo or something that I just made up, but knowing how these books have been written as a rapid inner dictation, I am sure if they were to try it—

G: And believe it, truly believe it—then miracles abound.

L: So what should we be saying to our children suffering from autism and similar afflictions to help with their transition out of them?

G: Be mindful of their likes and dislikes. Remind them of their "specialness" (of which we speak here only in human terms). "Unique" is perhaps a better word.

"You are unique and wonderful," not "You are behind other children (and always will be)."

"You move at your own pace," not "You will never catch up with the others."

L: Well, that's what we are saying to them, but what could parents or family and friends be doing in terms of internal phrasing to help lead them out of this eventually (if it truly is possible)?

G: And it is. Spark the fire by saying, "I am a child of God and all of the Universe. There are no words to describe one who has "lost their mind," because there is no such thing in the kingdom of heaven. For all who know that this is not a choice made prior but rather a circumstance from which to heal may begin to see my child as perfect and beautiful just as we all are. May all children grow out of this circumstance and be reminded of who they truly are by all in choir in their houses, schools, and communities. Amen."

L: What a beautiful prayer. I wish so badly that people would read this and really have this resonate with them. Is this why these types of things happen? Because we view each other as the labels put upon us, which are brought about by our fearful notions as an individual and collective consciousness?

G: Precisely accurate and, may we add, a miraculous presentation of spiritual facts.

L: May I ask, though, about my cousin? So what you are telling me here about my two-and-a-half-year-old cousin who had leukemia but is now a healthy, happy teenager is that the cause of her illness was the consciousness surrounding her? Do we choose circumstances such as getting sick as children (in order to heal ourselves miraculously) as a means to grow and evolve our soul?

G: Miraculous healing occurred here, did it not?

L: It did.

G: So why question a miracle?

L: Because I want to know if my cousin's soul chose this or if it was caused—

G: By chaos?

L: I would put it differently, but yes, that was my question.

G: Wherever chaos rains, be it conscious or subconscious, the floods eventually arrive for any and all in its path.

L: So if minds are never wasted in a spiritual sense, then depression or bipolar disorder is always—

G: Always.

L: A created circumstance.

G: Yes.

L: What about those crazy, ultrarare occasions when someone has a disease that only a handful of people on earth get?

G: On earth, as you are in heaven, may all minds be bound across (and between) time and space. Perhaps said circumstance has been bound to them from another realm. While instinctively one knows this is possible, all notions will be cast aside by readers of this material and truth will forever be lost. This is, however, very much your truth, all of your truths. It is entirely possible for afflictions of another realm to cross through to another. Although rare, it is plausible from a standpoint of universal concepts.

L: How does this happen?

G: We are glad you asked rather than dismiss this notion. One needs to remember all lifetimes are happening simultaneously in different portions of the vast, vast universe, which limited minds cannot and will not inscribe upon here or in other materials. It bears noting each lifetime affects all others—the sum of all parts, so to speak. So if one were to, say, witness an affliction in another realm, why, then it becomes possible for this to remain deeply rooted in the psyche, which ego mind traps in its claws.

L: How would we release all the "junk" our egos collect along the way in all our lifetimes?

G: You make a brilliant analogy when you speak of it this way. Bravo. Whoever undertakes practiced stillness and quiet contemplation with the maker releases any and all demons hiding beneath the surface. Those wishing to release these may say, "Dear God and All of the Universe, together shall we remain unbound to all perceived illnesses in any and all realms of existence in our nation and upon our planet and universal planes. Here shall we release to the nothingness all notices of separation. Amen."

L: This is wild. Truly wild. Yet it does make some sense. Oh my goodness, people are really going to think I am nuts. It's crazy to me as I write it here; I would never ever think this way, nor would I want to write this. It will upset so many. Yet somewhere deep inside of me I must know it's true because I can't seem to go back and erase it all.

G: Though it is your free will to do so. Go within, and remind yourself of your true nature in a deep meditation, and these truths shall come to light.

L: You know I cannot meditate well. This book is my meditation.

G: Thus, you have just proven our point. Whenever one is in deep meditation and capable of blocking out the world around and outside, then shall the truths be revealed. One who is bold and brave enough in body form will share these truths. One who is fearful of shame and ridicule will delete or not reveal these concepts to the world.

L: Well, I must be crazy, because I am going to share this. Why on earth would I ever write something like that? Why would those words come into my head and so quickly? What would be the point unless it was actually the truth? If it resonates, great. If it doesn't, move on to the next thing.

G: Perfection. Absolute perfection.

L: What about all these terrible allergies both kids and adults are now suffering from more recently? Peanuts, tree nuts, gluten, etc.

G: Have we not shown you how all minds in choir may affect another? Although the current bastardization of your world's food supply is at cause here as well. There is no rightful justification for the mindful pursuit of polyethylene as a means to package food products.

L: So there is an issue with chemicals seeping into our food supplies?

G: Yes. Privatization of food supply should never be encouraged. For only those willing to claim rights to food packaging shall be enraged here. However, spiritual principles aside for a moment, your endless supply of chemical concentrations in mass quantities are draping our foods in harmful substances, which no body (of a human form) is capable of processing. Corporations are at best feeding a famine by ethical manipulations of food supply here. Your processed food industries rely upon these concentrations of chemicals to quote "feed the hungry," but in spiritual reality (returning our conversation to that) there is no good reason to manipulate mass consumption products. Our planet is perfectly capable of housing, feeding, and clothing all of its inhabitants as long as necessary for their spiritual enlightenment.

L: Yet we don't do this. We let families and children go hungry each and every day on our planet. Meanwhile, the rich get richer, and the poor are taxed with doing all the grunt work to get the food out of the factories and to the poor families. But how can we fix this broken system so we can put an end to these types of allergies and allergens affecting our society en masse?

G: You are all at the effect of their cause. This is to say, "As one thinks, so shall all be."

L: Because they are knowing ethically and morally they are poisoning us slowly. This is why we get sicknesses and certain cancers?

G: Precisely. There are other factors as well, such as one's level of anxiety and stress. Consumption of alcoholic beverages and narcotics are at play here as well in terms of cancer causation. It is like the perfect storm of disease factors for one who drinks, smokes and lights up a microwave. This is not to say one's own mind processes are not also at play, as whenever a chosen circumstance has not been encountered, all who come seeking salvation may find this in prayer and practiced quietude.

L: But can we go back to the allergy situation we were first discussing?

G: Yes. We may.

L: Let me just ask simply: what is the cause of the allergies?

G: As we have explained here, the global causation occurs whenever a breakdown of ethical/moral codes is highlighted. Those in choir (your corporations seeking to profit wildly) are bound to a rule of the Universe that states all who speak, shall seek.

L: What does that mean, "All who speak, shall seek"?

G: Think of your ego mind like a race car. You rev your engines, and lights line up. You are ready to take off to the finish line. The flag gets raised, the engines roar, and the race begins. The all of the all of you are in competition with one another. Whenever one pulls ahead, another seeks to join or surpass that racer. Those who speak the loudest are often those in cahoots with corporate sponsorships.

L: I am so lost right now. I don't understand how this relates at all.

G: Loud speakers. Winner takes all.

L: So whoever wins the race is usually the—

G: One with the most backers. Money talks. We remind readers here that money is a magnet. So whoever throws the most money in the ring will ultimately come out on top. Although there is always free will, (which is the origin of your so-called underdog stories), in most cases, if not all, the Law of Attraction is at play here: that which is like unto itself is drawn[2].

L: I still do not understand how this all relates to how allergies are becoming more and more prevalent in our nation.

G: Your national crisis is directly related to the unending ethical and moral violations of your corporations and their CEOs and profiteers.

L: But I would imagine they are not doing this purposefully but rather subconsciously?

G: Yes, in that what they don't know will "kill" them; as in their deep-rooted subconscious fears about what is being done to the food supply are at best harming our bodies and at worst leading to all notions of separation and insanity.

L: Explain what you mean by that please.

G: "I'm better than you are. Therefore, I have no responsibility to you."

L: They don't care about the little people?

G: No. They care about profits and performance. Care not who eats; care only who consumes.

L: Meaning?

G: Consumerism is the name of the game. By whatever means possible shall we share more so that we may get more.

L: At the cost of our health? So is it the food per se or the ethical violations and subconscious thoughts being subjugated to all minds that are responsible for the rash of allergies in our current world view?

G: It is both cause and effect.

L: Well, how can we fix an obviously broken system?

G: Remind yourself of the true nature of reality, and remove all known carcinogens from your planetary system.

L: Sadly, that is easier said than done. That's not happening right now. So let's go to some practical advice for those dealing with food allergies. What can one say to help with this issue?

G: One must remind oneself of his or her dual nature—both mind/body and spirit and then, cocreate a new experience whereby all mindful issues are wiped away slowly through practices of meditation and mediation of all minds surrounding one another. You are at cause! You are at cause! You are at cause!

L: And now we are making jokes about *The Oprah Winfrey*[3] *Show*. Is this a "You get a car! You get a car! You get a car!" joke?

G: We are joking. Yes. The point being that in order to change one's mind on a subject such as autism, allergies, and other mindful afflictions, all in choir must be at choice to view that which is true and not that which is untrue.

L: Is this in terms of everything? Cancer too?

G: Yes. Those who are at cause must remind all in choir of who they really are as well.

L: But my little cousin did get better, and kids do grow out of allergies, and we are finding modalities to help those with autism.

G: Precisely our point here. This is why the need for "cures" is so important upon your planet. A "cure" for anything is the surest way to remind those in choir of healing capabilities. Believe in a cure, and this is what you all will see.

L: OK, I think I get it. It goes back to the biology of belief. If we all believe kids grow out of it, if we believe the medicine works or on the flip side that someone is "terminal," then all the minds in choir are just exacerbating the problem or engaging in the solution at hand.

G: Yes, for this is why we do say take the medicine and see the doctor, as these are healing modalities at the core, which come from a space of love. Those seeking to find cures will find them. Those seeking to profit will prolong the problem.

L: Is there a cure for cancer already?

G: Of course. The All of the All knows this.

L: I mean in terms of a medical cure?

G: Same answer. Do you fear this is an untruth?

L: Nope. Not at all. This is one thing we do agree on. I am fairly confident it is the truth. Someday, decades from now, a movie will be made about who kept it a secret and how.

G: Indeed.

L: What of someone who has been diagnosed as terminal,

like my brother? Was his stomach cancer a circumstance or a choice made prior?

G: Circumstance.

L: So he caused his cancer through his thoughts, words and actions?

G: Insomuch as he believed in all the medical mumbo jumbo and the corporate chaos: a perfect storm of mass manipulation.

L: You mean "mass" as in tumor. Very funny.

G: We are simply making light of the situation here as a way to remind you of the unreality of your brother's cancer diagnosis.

L: If a doctor had not deemed him "terminal," could he have lived or beaten cancer?

G: Yes. He who diagnoses the disease determines the damage. Those in a space of healing (doctors, scientists) would do well to remember this whenever delivering life-altering news.

L: This makes me so angry. I could have saved my brother (and maybe my dad from suicide) if I, if they, had known these universal truths.

G: For this was not your journey, and you would do well to remember this along your way so that you may use it as fuel to help others and not harm yourself with negative thinking and past regression. Do not let the mistakes of the past (of body) determine the future (of body-mind-soul). Thou shalt begin again and again and again until your life cycle upon earth (in its current incarnation) is done.

L: Can I help though? Is there anyone I can save who has been given a terminal diagnosis? I couldn't save my brother, but can I save others?

G: It is not up to you to "save" anyone. It is, however, upon you and all other beings of light and love to be reminded consistently of Love's presence in your life as a body. That is all one may do. Healing of oneself is one's only true remedy.

L: But can I be the one who helps remind them?

G: You shall always answer the call of those who come knocking. Those who speak, shall seek. However, you must know that you will see some return to the kingdom and some who are willing to remember. In these moments, it is upon our soldiers of spiritual wisdom to not internalize or demonize themselves whenever those who seek spiritual growth and enlightenment return to their prior ways of feeling lost and afraid. For not all are capable of "saving" themselves.

L: I am still not sure what "all who speak, shall seek" refers to. Can we break it down further and really get to the heart of its core message please?

G: Those who speak—the all of the all of you. Shall seek—enlightenment. Upon all is the rule of the universe, which states that those in body (the speakers) are also seekers longing for enlightenment.

L: OK, I get that, but how does this relate to the racing story and corporations?

G: Those who speak (the corporate profiteers) shall seek (riches and rewards). Whenever one is in chorus with ego, said law has been breached so that seekers seek ego gratification rather than spiritual gratification.

L: This is the same for the law of attraction, which is why it works for anyone who knows the principles?

G: Yes. Manifestations of wealth and abundance may come along once one understands this spiritual law (the same as gravity). This does not mean one manifesting riches is rightly returning to spiritual energy. Rather are they bound by the laws of the universe, which state that which is like unto itself is drawn. Draw upon these laws, and you may be rewarded richly, but not spiritually, until you relinquish all earthly possessions as necessary only for survival upon your planet rather than a necessity to one's ego pursuits.

L: And the same goes for all who speak, shall seek?

G: Yes, all who speak (the all of the all of you) are welcome to do and say whatever you want, for that is your free will. Seek, and you shall find what it is you are searching for in all manners of existence, be it spiritual or not. You get what you get because you spoke and thought of it.

L: I think I get it.

G: We knew you would, eventually. For all who come seeking shall find. This is spiritual law.

L: Seek and ye shall find?

G: A biblical passage straight from Source. Seek riches, find riches. Some are seeking enlightenment. Some are not. We are not here to blame or reward. We are all bound by the laws of our current universe. We are simply reminding those who wish to be reminded of their true nature. It is upon all bodies to decide what they seek to enhance their lives—be it gold or glory.

L: Let's go back to bodies. Is cancer always a circumstance, or is it a chosen affliction?

G: It is both.

L: Why? Why would a soul choose this for itself?

G: To grow and evolve one's soul is a complicated process of doing and undoing. Perhaps it is best to say that a choice made prior to leave the earthly plane, by one's soul, has many, many layers, which may be hard to ascertain or explain at the level at which you are all currently living. Therefore, we would simply say that all who seek to know God shall decide in which manner to leave the earthly plane, and for some, a cancer is a decision made along the way as a means to evolve both emotionally and physically. For such a diagnosis is rightly a terrible, tragic circumstance, and those in choir are rarely ever involved in ending sensations. It is, therefore, an "easy way out," so to speak, and a means to "say your goodbyes" rather than an abrupt ending, such as what has befallen several acquaintances of yours and their friends.

L: So our souls choose cancer as a way to die to help those who will be left behind to come to grips with what is happening?

G: Yes.

L: As opposed to an abrupt or tragic ending, which rips a family apart instantaneously?

G: Yes. Though their souls are also at choice in this manner as a means to evolve and grow experientially.

L: Can I talk to my soul and make sure we are in agreement on our ending?

G: Yes. You are always capable of extending your stay on the earthly plane. A soul, however, has a plan for you; as has been made by you for you.

L: Can we connect to this in quietness?

G: And contemplation, yes. Always.

L: So ultimately, we can be setting intentions, saying affirmations, meditating, etc., but if our soul has an agenda that differs from our ego's, we are going to find it hard to break that chain?

G: It is not necessary for you to break the chain, as you say. You are always at cause and are, therefore, capable of cocreating in any instant a new circumstance once you are understanding there is no separation.

"I am a soul in a body, and together we create a life of grandeur whereby all prior incarnations' manifestations are released and relinquished so that we may begin again and again and again."

L: We essentially have to make sure we are connecting back with our soul at all times, then. Is whatever happens part of their families', friends', or coworkers' soul journeys as well? Like, is it part of my journey to have lost my dad and brother and some friends along the way?

G: Of course. All journeys are intertwined here on earth and in heaven and other places and realms.

L: Do families reconvene? Are they always together?

G: Yes and no.

L: Well, which part is yes, and which is no?

G: Yes, in that you have always been and always will be, (I am) and therefore, your growth of soul mingles with other individual souls whenever you are at choice to be in a body or similar form or function. No, in that in each particular lifetime you may not always reconvene with the same souls, as this is again a part of your dual nature of love versus fear. Whom or what you encounter is guided by these two factions.

L: So which souls we wind up hanging out with again depends on what space we are coming from, love or fear?

G: Precisely. Yes.

L: Thank you as always for your wisdom and guidance. Now let us move on to the next thing so we can upset a few million more people. Many times, I have wanted to ask this question, and since we are speaking of illness, I guess now is a good time to pray about it.

"As we continue to create more books and material, may truths be revealed for all who seek them, including me. For I myself am not yet still a master of my inner world and, therefore, seek to inform others with my own questions. Amen."

You always write these for me, don't you?

G: That we do. As always, we are cocreators. We write as one mind. What is your burning question?

L: We spoke about Dr. Peebles—

G: We did—

L: In our last book. During a reading with a medium/channel, the medium told me through Dr. Peebles (a physician who died 100 years ago and is capable of being channeled) that my dad, after he died from suicide, was in some place called The Hospital of the Heart and Soul. Is that a place that actually exists?

G: Very much so.

L: What is it?

G: It is the mind's creation whenever those wishing for spiritual enhancement are returned to the maker.

L: Meaning?

G: Meaning when one reincarnates back to Source Energy, often times they are confused and deranged by what has just occurred. One's mind then instantaneously creates for itself a circumstance whereby that person is helped to remember their truths. Places such as this exist as sanctuaries for sanity until disorientation is healed.

L: Is that always the name for it—Hospital of the Heart and Soul?

G: It is not necessary to inscribe its proper name, only to address a concept of healing, metaphysically, which all who suffer upon reentry to Source Energy undertake either immediately or through no fault of their own.

L: What do you mean by "through no fault of their own"?

G: They are guided there whenever disorientation occurs as we have just told you.

L: How long would someone need to stay there?

G: As long as it takes. Some mere days, others minutes or months. We remind your readers that time-space in the kingdom is irrelevant. So our explanation is relevant only to your current time/space continuum on earth.

L: How long was my dad there?

G: Why don't you ask him?

L: I can't. May you please slow down? You are speaking too far ahead, almost thinking my thoughts for me.

G: We may. We do tend to get ahead of ourselves, for we are already knowing what it is you want to ask before you ask it here. You may ask your father the question now. You are scared?

L: I am.

G: Why?

L: Because I don't think I can connect to him.

G: Of course you can. We are all here always. Go ahead.

L: Dear God, please release this fear as I attempt to speak with my dad and gain answers from him now.

G: And what do you see?

L: Memories of times we had when I was younger and the time he interrupted my college graduation ceremony to take a cell phone call. Oh, and his giant cell phone on the beach when I was a teenager.

G: This is how all who crossed relate—the sharing of memories and good (God) moments in time.

L: So this is how psychics do readings? They see those memories?

G: Precisely. The ringing in your left ear, this is us. (We like that show very much, you know. It is a masterpiece of TV making.)

L: It's very subtle, but I do hear it. I hadn't noticed it until now. Was it always there when we were communicating in the last book?

G: The link is stronger than ever between us all. Do you wish to commune with your father more now?

L: Yes. What may I ask him?

G: Anything you want. Go on.

L: Is he happy?

Dad: Absolutely.

L: Do you miss me?

Dad: More than you know.

L: Why can't I see you again?

Dad: It's not allowed.

L: What about Jason? Is he there with you?

Dad: Please don't cry.

L: I can't help it.

Dad: I gave you a message last week through Corey; I know you received it.

My friend Corey had visited a psychic medium who relayed a message from my dad during her reading.

L: I did. I knew it was for me.

Dad: I am not the man I used to be. I have studied. I have remedied all of the past mistakes. I have shared my heart, and I am with you always. Your pain is mine. Your triumph is mine. My love is yours always for you. We are with you always.

L: What about Jason?

Dad: He is here.

Jason: Sister!

My brother used to always emphatically call me "sister" as a joke instead of my name.

L: Are you together?

Jason: Always. In a way that you can't understand, but yes, we are together, never separate. I see Kim. I see you and Max and your dog.

L: I'm not sure whether or not to erase this all. It just doesn't feel right to me.

Dad: You are talking to God for goodness sake. You think you can't talk to us too?

G: Fear holds you back. Often times speaking to relatives of a familial nature (we are all related in the kingdom) can be more difficult, as sorrow holds us back.

L: How can I talk to them more consistently?

Jason: Just ask.

L: This feels wrong and strange and untruthful. Is my ego perhaps playing tricks on me right now?

G: Not at all. Your dad is here. Your grandma, cousin, brother, an aunt, a sister (you don't remember in this lifetime), your dog's Raven and Paris and the man murdered in Cuba, the caretaker of your life for a while until your brother arrived.

L: And Albert, the young man who died in Cuba, was my guardian angel? I have always thought that. I had a car accident once, and I was positive that was who saved my life. I felt as if he were literally—

G: Figuratively.

L: Sitting in the seat next to me, calming me down. It was a miracle I was not killed in that car accident. It was raining, and I hit a guard rail; my car slid across five lanes of the freeway during morning rush hour, and yet not one car hit me. I landed in a ditch. As I sat there crying, I felt at peace almost and as if Albert were there with me.

G: Is this Albert you were thinking of or perhaps someone else?

A memory of my friend Patrick who died in college flashed in my mind.

L: Wait. Wow. Oh my goodness! Was it Patrick? That thought just came to me.

G: Yes, it was Patrick. Albert died many years later.

L: Oh my goodness, yes. I forgot about Patrick, but you are right; Albert was still alive when that happened. Holy cow. I would have never remembered that on my own.

G: Do you see how subconscious thoughts work and why they must be released through meditation or other focused modalities?

L: They got locked away. My memories were locked away. I have not thought about Patrick in so many years. Where is he?

G: He is in another form, in another dimension, learning, growing, and evolving as all of the all often do.

L: So if people who lived on earth cross back over to Source Energy "die," how long do they stay there? At what point do they decide to return? For example, if my dad or brother decides to incarnate into another dimension, would I no longer be able to communicate with him? I thought our loved ones were with us always. At least, this is what I have always told people, as it's what I thought happens.

G: You are not incorrect in the assumption that your loved ones are with you always. You are, however, misinformed in thinking they are in body form always.

L: What do you mean by that?

G: Meaning even if they are in body form somewhere else, they are still with you metaphysically. Though you do not remember, you too are here always.

L: I am? Part of our soul stays with Source Energy?

G: Yes. Do you think if the Creator can create unto itself another, you cannot do this as well?

L: So in energy form—

G: This is how there can be multiples *yous* in all parts of our vast expansive universe and cosmos. This is the no thing of which you all exist. You are not one thing; you are no thing.

L: Meaning what?

G: No thing meaning you are not one, you are all.

L: I really don't understand.

G: You are not all, and you are not separate from the all. A soul divided is a soul united. All for one, one for all. This is it. This is truth.

L: This is, whoa. My soul, then, is an energy split into billions—

G: Trillions upon trillions; soul is infinite.

L: My soul can be split into—

G: What you are not understanding here is that we are all one being, of one mind. Nowhere have you not been. No one have you not been. You are you. You are me. You are we. Wherever we are, you are. You are here, there, and everywhere all at once.

L: I guess I understand. No, actually, I don't.

G: This is why we are here always to explain the truths of the universe, as difficult as they may be to transcribe or inscribe. We are all one. We are with you. We are in you. We are you. Frustration stops the flow. It is not necessary to understand these concepts as truth. Eventually all will come to know truth. While we appreciate this time spent in cocreation, much of what we inscribe here will be impossible to decipher for the reader and inscriber. This is why we ask all who are seekers and sharers of this information to return to it over and over, many, many times. The more one reads and relates, the closer will they come to knowing universal truths. We are all one being. You are a soul seeking to know itself experientially. For this is why all experiences are happening at once—so you may see through the puzzle pieces.

L: I have heard this, that life is one giant puzzle, a mystery waiting to be solved.

G: If you don't mind a puzzle with infinite pieces, infinite parts waiting to be discovered and assembled.

L: So my soul is hanging out in all parts of the universe?

G: And cosmos, yes.

L: But is also part of—

G: Source Energy. Yes! This is how we are able to explain you are all God. There is nowhere you are not and no one you are not.

L: So it goes back to this question: am I talking to God or not?

G: You are talking to we. You are we. Your truth is our truth is their truth. We are all one giant being of light split into billions upon trillions of infinite parts. We are the sum of all parts. We are God/Universe/Source, the All of Everything. You are your dad, your brother, your uncle, your grandfather, and your best friend. You are Albert and Patrick and Kristy (your friend who died many years ago). You are John and Bob and Kate and Kelly, strangers in body form but brethren in spirit form.

L: So this is how I am talking to God? We are we. So I can sit here in body form and essentially talk to my own soul, which is all of us together in energy form? As body forms we are separate. As spirits we are united?

G: Insomuch as anytime you are "of body" but also re-minded back with the Oneness; then any one of you may talk to God (the word that has been inscribed in this material), as you are all part of and apart from God.

L: But only if you are in a high state of awareness and belief can you do such a thing?

G: Yes. Those who are aware of Source Energy and concepts related to the metaphysical may connect with their guides, angels, and inner souls anytime they are reminded back with the Oneness.

L: So can you explain, then, if we are all one being, how can I as an individual soul have lived 772 lifetimes as you told me I had in our first book? If we all come from Source Energy and are individuated into a soul, wouldn't I be infinite souls and infinite lifetimes?

G: Yes.

L: So I am confused, then, about the 772 lifetimes.

G: We shall explain it like this. Whenever one has made the choice to individuate one's soul, they are therefore, then separated from Source. This does not mean, however, that you are separate from Source, as we are all one giant being of light and love. However, one's consciousness is capable of separating itself among the cosmos.

L: I don't get it right now. Perhaps we can tackle this later or in other material and at some point I will understand what you mean.

G: Your confusion is warranted here, and for this we would say to the all of you that much of what we are writing here goes against what has been taught in your uncivilized society, and therefore, whoever undertakes focused intention to gain the answers within will decide whether or not these notions are truthful. We can, however, tell you—right here, right now—there is nothing you cannot be, do, or have, and therefore, the all of you are capable of understanding all of this once you are ready. You are simply not ready to hear and comprehend these truths.

L: Can I ask, then, if when my dad and brother died, were they greeted by my soul as well? Was I there with them in a sense?

G: In body form, yes. This is how all who cross relate in body form. It will feel as if you too are still in body form until disorientation has occurred and subsided. Once you are understanding of the dual nature of consciousness, you will then disappear back to the nothingness and become one with all of the Universe.

L: So I was there too with my dad in The Hospital of the Heart and Soul?

G: Yes. Until the understanding of who and what you truly are is occurring, you are with loved ones always. Once recognition of self occurs, you have no need for those in body form. You merge back into one.

L: But can't we also be separated as souls in heaven when we die?

G: Absolutely. You are both everything and nothing at all.

L: I think I get this concept somewhat. I'm not sure how to truly believe in this since obviously none of us on earth have ever seen this, and there is no proof, but I think I

understand. When we are in a body form, we can be a separate consciousness and, at the same time, part of the collective consciousness. When we cross over or die, we can still be a separate consciousness but also part of Source Energy?

G: Yes, with the only difference being you are no longer living within the illusion and are, therefore, able to comprehend fully our Oneness.

L: Then what? Where do we go from there?

G: You either make the choice to individuate your soul again and again or you remain with Source as angels or guides.

L: Yes, but if we are all one, why would someone be my guide or guardian angel? This doesn't make sense. Couldn't I just help myself?

G: Yes, insomuch as you are helping yourself as the body that you have been in your lifetime. If you are Albert (your coworker) and you are Stuart (your dad) and you are Jason (your brother), then any one of them may be your guide because they too are part of you. Your thinking from ego's perspective allows you to believe it is Albert or Jason or Stuart who is helping you, but in actuality it is all of us together.

L: I still don't understand that concept right now. Let's move on. You mentioned guides; can we go back to Albert, then, please?

G: We may. You felt it, we know. Your guide's presence?

L: I did. Yes. I had a feeling; but I also had a psychic medium bring it up in a reading one time, someone who beyond a shadow of a doubt would have not known who Albert was in relation to my life. Yet the medium was perfectly accurate with every detail of how he died. It was one of those moments where I could not deny that there is a place we go when we die.

G: There is. Right here back in the loving arms of God and the Universe.

L: Our guides exist. What about angels? Do they exist?

G: Of course. You are all a part of the All of Everything. It is only in body form where you are separated. So "angel" is simply a term for anyone who is presently not "of body."

L: So anyone who has decided to not return to a body or a similar form?

G: Yes. Remarkable explanation.

L: So angels do not walk among us as some have said they do?

G: No, insomuch as they are not "angels" upon your planet but rather bodies whose minds are closer to God's mind.

L: I think I get that. "Angels" in heaven are those who have chosen to stay in nonphysical form—

G: After they have incarnated a multitude of experiential

circumstances and are certain of who they truly are, they then bind to the energy permanently.

L: And our souls are part of that energy but not permanently. So we split ourselves apart in order to grow and evolve our soul through experiences of equal and opposite polarities—good and bad, ugly and pretty, short and tall, nice and naughty, genius and dummy. Then what happens?

G: Then, when you are ready to return permanently to Source Energy, you are bound back with the Oneness where you may help others grow and evolve their souls.

L: Then it's not my brother or dad helping me throughout this lifetime. It's me?

G: This is not what we are saying. Here we are trying to explain how soul is re-created again and again throughout lifetime after lifetime in circumstance after circumstance. Whenever one's current lifetime ceases to exist based on thoughts, words, and actions or chosen circumstances, then may they return to the heavens immediately to be reunited with Source Energy where we are all one. As part of the Oneness, all shall remind themselves of who they truly are through focused awareness of all that has occurred within time and space of that particular incarnation. Once undertaken, then may they be reunited within their own souls and thus undertake a notion of guidance for others who have remained "of body." This is not to say you are not capable of helping yourself; you are. You all are. We are stating a case for that which is "of soul," which is to say that all souls are one soul. So you are helping each other as one.

L: I am so lost. I just don't get it. In one way, you are saying our souls help us, but in another you are saying our loved ones who died can help us. It seems contradictory to me. Is there a way of explaining that is simpler and won't fry my brain?

G: Your ego is at issue here, not your brain. Ego wishes to hold hostage anyone seeking universal truths and principles. Let go of ego. Let go of fear. Let go of separation. Miracles will occur when one is understanding of this concept.

L: So how could our loved ones who have died help us when we are in body form?

G: Do you know that your soul is right now helping those in body form too insomuch as you are and were a body in other lifetimes and those remaining "stick around" always to help them? The essence of the soul is around to guide them whenever they turn toward "God's" light (i.e., any thought that comes from love). Often times you are in a state of sorrow and feel as if they may be there with you. And they are. They are also in other places too, as are you.

L: Well, I am just totally and completely lost here, and I would imagine some people reading this are as well.

G: To comprehend something as vast and expansive can be quite literally an impossibility for irrational (ego) minds, which are consistently running the show. Whenever a notion of true connection and full-out belief is undertaken, then these concepts will resonate within one's soul. Until that time, be free of the burden of anger and frustration here. To know yourself is to know you are not without limitations when you are "of body." Stop trying to figure it all out, and remain open to the possibilities of which we have inscribed here. At some point, those who have focused their intentions toward a spiritual awakening will have all answers simultaneously.

L: Is it possible the further we go with this conversation or interview that I may actually get this?

G: It is without question a possibility, yes, should free will not take your focus away from the material at hand. We shall continue this material and conversation in depth much later on. First, let us return to your friend Albert, who was very much your "guardian angel," so to speak, until your brother was awakened back to Source.

L: I get my brother being my guardian angel but why Albert? Why would he have chosen to be my guardian angel? We were just coworkers, not super close, though I loved him dearly. He was a kind, sweet young man.

G: He has been your caretaker in many lifetimes before. His role on earth was of that, a caretaker. His affliction offered a clarity of truths for which he understood in this lifetime. He loved all and saw no one differently.

L: That is true. He really just exuded love and kindness. He was happy all the time.

G: His "specialness," which others saw as "slow" or "retarded," (a word that is bothering you right now but is perfectly acceptable here in relation to our conversation) was a choice made prior to incarnation. All who came upon him arrived for a reason.

L: Is this true of all the people we view as mentally challenged?

G: Yes, a choice made prior to advance one's soul from a place of love with no limitations. Born of fear, these highly advanced souls know nothing of hate, only love. It would do your world well to remember this and stop treating them as wonders of amusement but rather as beings of God's love.

L: But you stated earlier that "a mind we will never waste" about kids with autism, so this would seemingly contradict those who are born with something like Down syndrome. If an impacted mind is caused by the collective thoughts of all in choir with one another, how does this explain Down syndrome or other similar afflictions?

G: What if I told you there was nothing wrong with their minds?

L: I am not sure I would believe that. It would seem as if there is.

G: Yet they see only love. What have we been explaining to you for two whole books?

L: That only love is real.

G: So what does that tell you about those beings who have chosen to incarnate for purposes of growing and evolving their souls from a space of pure love?

L: We see there being something "wrong" with them.

G: But there is everything right with them. Perhaps those in choir are portraying in them characteristics that seek to enslave them, but in actuality they are very much perfect.

L: But certainly they have struggles, challenges, and upsets and are incapable of using their minds to return to the Oneness. You can't cure Down syndrome; at least I don't think you can.

G: Why would you want to?

L: So they may lead a more normal life.

G: Normal in the eyes of whom? What is normal? Is normal chasing money, fame, and all manners of self-denial and love? Or is normal loving exactly who you are where you are. You see normal as ego's lofty pursuits. We see normal as giving and sharing love unconditionally.

L: That makes me want to cry, and again I'm not sure if its tears of joy, sorrow, or both. But there is no cure and no way, even through prayer and intention and all the things we have been speaking about, to heal them.

G: This is simply not true, and though it would be seemingly miraculous, it is possible when all minds in choir around them begin to see them as perfect and whole already. Put an end to ungodly thoughts surrounding their condition, and remind them daily of who they truly are (whenever they are capable of comprehending an insane notion that is very much sane), and miracles abound. It will not be easy, as binding minds can and will be difficult to undertake for all those in choir surrounding these beautiful beings of light who are very much teachers to the all of you.

L: They are teachers to us?

G: Yes, and what would you say they teach?

L: I have not a clue.

G: Simply not true. Have a think on it, and get back to us.

Rainbows and Unicorns

" **D**ear God and All of the Universe, tonight we shall come together to continue sharing the truths of the Universe in great detail for all who come seeking to be reminded of inner truths. Amen."

Laura: I took a few days off from writing, and no answer really came to me on what those with Down syndrome may be teaching us.

God: That is OK. Let us first discuss today's rainbow you saw, and then we may go back to our earlier conversation.

L: Thank you for my rainbow today, by the way.

G: Why do you think those are possible?

L: From a scientific or spiritual level?

G: Spiritual, of course.

L: Well, lots of people saw it today. I wasn't the only one.

G: As we have said many times, in many ways, no one is more special than the next; simply are they more aware of Love's presence in their life. Those of a higher vibration are noticing when beauty is around them. Those of a lower vibration notice only deadlines looming.

L: Do you send us those rainbows?

G: Yes, of course we do.

L: Why?

G: Beauty is necessary to remind one of the nature of being. Human beings tend to miss the moments of life. Every once in a while, we must remind them of magnificence. Even the enlightened are uplifted by the sign of a rainbow. It is God's perfect symbol of restitution.

L: Restitution?

G: A way to remind us that we are capable of abundance in all manors of existence. For whenever a rainbow is above head, remember this.

L: Is this why we say there is a "pot of gold" at the end of the rainbow?

G: Precisely. Be it financial gain, emotional drainage, or relieving any other cyclical patterns of abuse, a pot of gold at the end of a rainbow is always available unto thee. Here shall I release any and all behavioral patterns of ego's abuse and remind myself of magic.

L: Not all places are capable of seeing rainbows all the time. In California, for example, it doesn't rain all summer.

G: Perhaps we have more than one trick up our sleeve.

L: Tell me something else that brings these magical messages.

G: Unicorns.

L: Well, we don't see them in everyday life. They are not real.

G: They are real; very much so. What must be known is while they cannot be viewed from a human's perspective, these creatures of great beauty exist and forever are symbols of mystery and magic. Seeing one in a photograph, billboard, magazine page, or internet post carries the same message as the rainbow.

L: Will you show me one today?

G: Of course. Then it is upon you to let it go and not denigrate into fear via the ego. It is in the let go where all great manifestations occur. For only in the let go can an ego mind be released. Think not, have not.

L: Think not, have not?

G: Think not of what you can't create but rather of what you can create. Think not of unicorns not showing up in your experience but rather that unicorns will show up. Your will is our will. Your "have not" is a sure sign of lack. That which you are lacking is that which you feel you have not. Make sense?

L: As always, yes.

G: Let us return to your questions of those who humans deem "retarded."

L: What would a proper word be in God's terminology?

G: Beings of wonder. Shiners of truths of evolutionary patterns whereby those of a lesser intelligence are ridiculed and shamed rather than revered for their abilities to see love only where there is fear.

L: So then they are teaching—

G: Unconditional love. To love unconditionally is the true nature of all beings upon your planet and others. The mentally challenged as has been coined for a more appropriate term among your humans of earth, are "special" in that they are highly evolved beings. Though from a spiritual perspective, no one is more special than the next, from an evolutionary standpoint their special magic is that they see only magic and wonderment. Their lives are full of rainbows and sunshine always.

L: Is this why we call them "special" as humans?

G: Precisely. Though it is a term of a derogatory nature assigned by humans and other species to these highly evolved souls, it is quite accurate as an evolutionary concept.

L: So there is nothing wrong with them?

G: There is everything right about them. Beautiful souls who undertake (incarnate) an experience like no other and who seek only to remind those in their worlds of love, kindness, joy, and magic.

L: Wow. So the rainbow I saw today was meant to stir up this conversation where, a couple of days ago, you asked me to think about what the mentally challenged are teaching us.

G: Was it not more beautiful than the last rainbow you saw, and did you not feel the notion of wanting to write in your book today?

L: It was particularly beautiful today, yes.

G: Things have a way of working themselves out, don't they? This is a metaphor for all of life. When in doubt, look for the rainbows, the unicorns, and the messages of love and kindness surrounding the all of you always.

L: Why can I write this book and know these words are not my own but still question and doubt all of this? Why is it so hard to get rid of irrational thoughts?

G: You are still looking for your own pot of gold.

L: What do you mean?

G: We are glad you asked. We have been waiting for this discussion.

L: OK, lay it on me.

G: You are not yet ready to hear your truth.

L: But I want to hear it even if I am not ready.

G: You are richer than you know.

L: Meaning?

G: You are rich with love, laughter, and friends; you are rich monetarily, physically, and in all manners of form and function.

L: Meaning?

G: Nothing is ever good enough for you. Your home is either too large or too small. Your bank account is full, yet you refuse to spend it. Your body is strong, yet you focus on weakness. Your children are coming, yet you refuse to believe it. You are your own worst enemy in manners of form and function which simply means stop dwelling upon that which you do not have. Dwell upon that which you do have. All that you have is enough. More comes once we own this truth. That which you are is that which you have been and always will be. Quit while you are ahead.

L: Quit while I am ahead? I don't understand how that relates?

G: You already have that which you are desiring in this and other lifetimes. Quit focusing on that which you do not have, and focus on that which is in front of and beside you. All you need is available to you forever and always whenever you focus upon love and not lack. Love what you have. Bless it.

L: I think I understand what you are saying, but I feel as though it's easier said than done, especially when it comes to financial issues. Remember that the 1 percent has all the wealth and the 99 percent is always scraping by or living at or above its means.

G: The 1 percent has figured out the secret sauce of life. Give. Get. Receive. Give monetarily, get monetarily, and receive monetarily. The cycle starts again. Give. Get. Receive. Give a million dollars. Get a million dollars. Receive millions more.

L: Yes but in our last book you said giving to receive in order to get is not actually giving at all.

G: And here we are saying this is not spiritually uplifting; we are only making the point that your ego, whenever it is running the show, is always capable of creating wealth, albeit not of a spiritual kind. What the 1 percent lacks in emotional wealth is far superior to what they have gained in financial wealth. Whenever one seeks to profit and gain only from a financial perspective, then they are missing the growth of soul, which, as we have told you, is part of your purpose on earth and in heaven. Giving to get in order to receive merely makes them more capable of financial wealth in this incarnation; it also, however, guarantees in related incarnations that one will perhaps be homeless. Let us remind all that to know oneself is to know oneself experientially as all things. You must be the all of everything in order to achieve master status as a sentient and spiritual being.

L: So you are saying someone who is crazy rich right now will be totally poor in another lifetime?

G: For all things, for all souls.

L: Well, if you are meant to experience both things, yin and yang, as you said in our first book, are people who are homeless capable of pulling themselves out of that by cocreating with the Universe a new experience?

G: Available to all of you are we always. If one has chosen for this go-round, so to speak, a circumstance whereby they find themselves homeless or poor, they always have the choice "of body" to remind themselves of that which they came from, which is unconditional love. It is not necessary to stay in said circumstance permanently. You have simply chosen to experience said notion of what it means to be poor. Once this has been experienced in that lifetime, be it five days, years, or minutes, one is capable of recreating a new pattern of thought. You do this, as we have reminded the all of you, by returning to your maker and proclaiming, "I no longer wish to be poor. I desire a new result of which I know I am capable, as it already exists as possibility for me. As the All of Everything, there is nothing I have not been in all circumstances of existence. Therefore, that which I am desiring is available unto me."

Then it is upon you all to focus on that which you do already have in the here and now so that you may not keep away that which is available and coming to you. Do you understand? We know our explanations may be lengthy and difficult to inscribe and translate.

L: I think I do understand. It does make sense for the most part except that I feel that getting and receiving are the same thing. May you please clarify?

G: They are different in that *get* is a transitive verb. It is an action one takes. Getting, in this context, is to go out and obtain.

Receiving comes through law of magnetic attraction. That which you have obtained attaches back to itself more and more.

L: Thank you.

G: We are always available to you, to all of you.

L: Still no unicorn yet!

G: It's coming. That which is like unto itself is drawn is a law of the universe. Whatever you focus your attention upon is what will grow in your experience. This is why it is always best to focus one's awareness upon that which they choose to see and not what is unkind or unfavorable.

L: Well speaking of unfavorable things, I was very upset to find another dead bird on my patio today. I understand the first one was a message of transformation and change. May you please interpret accurately for me the reason for the second bird?

G: May we ask that you close your eyes?

L: I saw a ray from the sun shining upon the bird, and I heard, "There is no death."

G: Very good. Try again. Focus your intention on receiving the answer within.

L: I saw the bird flapping its wings and flying away. And

I heard, "All creatures big and small are meant to bring messages of hope and love, be those creatures alive or dead."

So what is the message?

G: The same message of hope and love and change.

L: Can I make it stop though? I don't want dead animals to be my new license plates, which were my original signs when my spiritual journey first began.

G: You are absolutely correct. Though you are currently laughing, this is precisely how awareness works. That which is like unto itself is drawn. Your awareness upon the first bird created a circumstance whereby the second bird became a possibility. And how shall I stop this, you are wanting to ask.

L: Well, of course. I don't want any more dead birds on my watch. Can we please go back to license plates? Those are the best. Wait. Is this why I keep seeing rainbows? This was my third one in two weeks.

G: Ring the bell. You are learning.

L: I love rainbows. Let's keep those and the license plates. Oh, and the dragonflies and butterflies I always see. What would I say to get rid of the dead birds?

G: "Dear Great Father of heaven, I know now that where I put my awareness is precisely what will show up in my experience over and over again until I recognize it as either helpful or hurtful. As we seek, so shall we find the evidence of that which we are seeking. May we please release from my awareness all dead animals as a means of transformational messages. Amen."

L: And that's it?

G: That is all one needs to cocreate an experience, yes.

L: And I would imagine you are going to tell me that money works in the same way?

G: Of course, yet again, you know this answer, but we will indulge you once again. Money is a conduit for that which is necessary to grow and evolve human emotions and thoughts. Awareness placed upon lack will bring about more lack. Awareness placed upon that which you are desiring within your experience will bring about more and more of the desired element, be it money or cocoa beans. That which you feel you are lacking will serve to keep those things away from you.

"I want more money. I need to be rich. I can't afford this or that. I don't have enough." These are words of sacrifice.

L: Why would they be words of sacrifice?

G: We are glad you asked. Sacrificial words are those that seek to enslave ego's thinking mind.

"I never have enough. Nobody likes me. I can't ever be taken seriously. This shirt makes me look fat. I am ugly and unlikable."

These are ego's tricks for enslavement. Words of surrender are the following: I am. I have. I do. I can. I will, and I should.

L: "Should" doesn't seem to fit in with that. "Should" feels like a word of enslavement.

G: Fantastic. You are learning. For whenever an irrational thought is placed here, shall you question it, and we shall give you an answer. Should is a word that incites fear. For we have placed it here as a tool for deciphering that which is of ego and that which is of God. Thou should never refer to any worthy pursuit in life as a "should."

"I will do this. I can do this. Nothing will stop me from this. I am capable."

L: Yes, because if I say I should sell these books and help people, it implies a sense of annoyance at all the work that lies ahead of me. If I say it as I will sell these books and help people, it comes across as empowering and motivating.

G: A perfectly arranged example of a point we are making. Words of enslavement will always keep you stuck in cyclical patterns. Words of surrender are reminders of that which you are capable of doing and that which you are surrendering to God and all of the Universe.

I went about the rest of the day, and sure enough, I saw two unicorn photos.

L: Well, I have to say a big thank you for my unicorns.

G: Ask, and you shall receive. All upon your earth may be blessed with the same magic moments whenever right-minded thoughts align. Your will is our will. Your ask is answered always in circumstances arriving from thoughts of godliness. All are welcome to the spoils of wonder.

L: But what about those times when you are desiring something that you think is going to be amazing for you, and it doesn't happen? For example, there is a job that was a dream job, something you had wished for your entire life,

and you feel as though you have been taking the baby steps to make that dream a reality, but you don't get the job. How does someone reconcile that? If your whole life you say, "I can and I will," and it doesn't happen, what is the problem? If our will is your will, then what are we doing wrong? Do we want the wrong things? Is our ego running the show?

G: Whenever thoughts of ego enter the fray, any and all desires are pushed aside for loftier pursuits.

L: But I really wanted to be an entertainment reporter, and I wanted to be a host and have more exposure. Yet, as hard as I tried, it never seemed to happen where I could advance my career further than I got with *Access Hollywood*.

G: And why do you think that is? Do you think it was "our" decision, "our" guidance that led you astray?

L: Yes.

G: Why?

L: Because I feel now as if it was my soul's journey to be a speaker, healer, mentor, and teacher.

G: Do you feel this is not something you could have done had you not been able to achieve your loftier career goals?

L: I feel as though I didn't achieve those things, because there was a divine plan in place, which led me to writing these books and materials.

G: This may surprise you, but you are wrong in that assumption. The only reason for your lack of observational success in a chosen field is your lack of concentration on that portion of you, which subsequently desired a result. In your failure to see your own worthiness, you created an undesired result, feeling as if nobody wanted you. You see, my dear, nothing happens "at random" to you that doesn't happen through you. We have touched on this so many times before, and yet we will return again and again until all of the all of you truly grasp this concept. You are at cause for the all of everything that occurs in your current plane of existence (incarnation). Your failure to advance your career was nothing more than your own thought processes brought upon by ego's pursuit of something bigger and better. The bigger, better deal. This is a common problem in your world's view, both inner and outer.

L: We spoke of this in our last book. I could have become a famous TV host and still have been able to write these books one day?

G: Absolutely.

L: So then am I the cause or not the cause of these books?

G: Very good question. You are the cause of these books because of your thoughts, words, and actions. There is no one right way to know God, for we all take our paths to glory. These books existed as possibility, always, and therefore, in your knowing, you created them via your conscious choices.

L: But what about, as an example, if I take this book to a publisher and that door is a dead end, and another and another, and they wind up being dead ends, and then I take it to one publisher, and that publisher says yes. I feel as if those closed doors were closed for a reason, and the open door was open for a reason. Do you understand what I mean?

G: Yes, we understand completely. Yet what you must know is those closed doors were closed for a reason—your reasoning. In your guidance, your soul created circumstances of a closed door.

L: But whose guidance? God's? Spirit's? Angels'?

G: Yes, all of the above. Remember, for we are all one; so simple semantics explains this process.

L: So my soul and all of the Universe, God, and the angels knew what was best for me and—

G: Will give you exactly what you want or desire. In this particular issue, you both want and desire a result for your book. Whenever one is wanting a thing but there is not desire at play is when a closed door will feel like a locked coffin.

L: So this is when you are banging your head against a wall because something is not happening for it? It's not something our soul is truly desiring.

G: This is not to say that an ego's wants are not attainable; certainly they are whenever an absence of fear and doubting occurs.

L: Like if I want a pair of expensive shoes really badly and I work to get them and believe I will get the money for them.

My soul is not desiring them, but my ego is, and the law of attraction is at play here? I was able to draw it to me in my belief—

G: In your wanting and lack of doubting, you drew upon the universal system of energy. We get both what we want and desire whenever an absence of fear is undertaken. This is not to say these wants are good for the soul; we are merely reminding you these wants are always attainable through free will thinking. For what you are wanting is always attainable in the absence of fears as are all desires manifesting themselves as a soul's true calling.

L: So this is why we sometimes feel as if we have a calling to do or be something? Like being an author and writing these books was my calling. Was this a choice made prior to incarnation?

G: Yes. To grow and evolve your soul as a thought leader. For you have been this before in other lifetimes, as we have shown you in a playground discovery of a card on the ground.

L: Yes. I found a playing card on the ground, and it had a picture of a city called Perge in Turkey. I took it home with me because I felt as if it was a message for me. I kept it in a book.

G: It was for you. Intuitively you felt this, which is why you kept it and placed it in a book for safe keeping.

L: When I looked up Perge, I was drawn to the story of a woman named Matrona of Perge.

G: She (meaning a *you* in another lifetime) is a priestess of the high order. She was physically and mentally abused by her husband. Rightly she escaped to a monastery where she was taken in by a kindly monk who discovered her; she had bandages covering her lady parts.

L: So she tried to hide her bruises?

G: No. She was a he, or at least this is what all who came upon her believed. For she had bandaged herself to look as if she were a man and disguise her true identity. For many, many years she lived as this woman as if she were a man until she was discovered and exiled from the monastery for fear she would be imprisoned by religious leaders who at the time were bitter and angry about women in any amount of power, a rarity in those days.

L: Is that why I found that playing card on the playground that day? I was meant to know this is who I was in another incarnation?

G: In your asking, you received. Drawn to you was the unlocking of yet another circumstantial existence. First thought is the right thought. Yes, we have sent you many a clue that you have yet to decipher. More will come your way, and here shall we unlock them and in other materials as well.

L: Did she die, then, from circumstance or a choice made prior to incarnation?

G: For this we would have to explain that her choice was to remain "of body" for a lengthy period of time so as to enact change upon your planet.

L: This sounds awfully familiar. Yet again a similarity to something in my own life.

G: It is exactly as you thought.

No Doubt

"*Dear God, whenever I am holding on to fear, may we work toward releasing it here, and within these pages allow me to share my struggles so others may benefit from my experiences and be reminded of their true connection. Amen.*"

Laura: I had a rough couple of days where my ego was clearly in charge. I did what I had been told here, which was to pray in every instant for the thoughts to be removed. Sure enough, it finally started to work (though it took a solid twenty-four hours before I felt any better). Why can't we cast our egos aside permanently through prayer and intention?

God: You can in an instant with a prayer of restitution.

L: Which would be what?

G: "Dear God, may we please cast aside all ego musings so that we may share spiritual truths with all who come seeking the riches and rewards of reunification with Source Energy. Amen."

L: That's in any instant. I asked why can we not get rid of the ego permanently.

G: You can. However, when you are "of body" it does not benefit your body to do this. For there are moments of time when ego is at play that serve the systems of energy from which you all incarnated on your current planet.

"I am hungry. I need to eat. I would like a sandwich or a salad. I know not to crash my car into a light pole purposefully."

Many times, ego is at play and at odds with the soul. It is a marriage of both convenience and inconvenience.

L: Is our ego in charge in cases where someone has become violent?

G: Yes, unless it has been agreed upon prior that souls in a violent encounter may prey upon one another.

L: Preying upon one another? As in if we incarnate to kill another person?

G: Preying upon one another as in first, do no harm.

L: I am not understanding. May you please explain this better?

G: We may. To prey upon another being is to incite in that being a notion of such rage and anger that its only recourse is of a violent nature. To know oneself as incapable of rage, one must first know vengeance.

L: Well, I understand that notion, but what do you mean by "First, do no harm"?

G: Precisely as we have stated above. First, do no harm; then may the opposite be revealed unto you as a means to know yourself as the All of Everything.

L: Why would we want to know ourselves as angry, bitter, resentful, or vengeful?

G: What does it feel like to be loving and kind to others?

L: It feels good. I enjoy doing things for other people.

G: But how may you know this feeling of joy and elation if you don't know its direct opposite? You can't say fat if you have never known thin. Up or down, left or right, love or fear. To know oneself fully, one must know all things of an opposite reactionary nature.

L: I understand this, but I also feel as though this is perhaps part of the reason why our world is so messed up. We see accidents or vengeance, illnesses and afflictions, lives cut short and reported on by the media, or people posting about negative things on social media. How would one know if someone has chosen this circumstance or created it so that it doesn't spread like a virus into our subconscious thoughts? I had a friend in high school whose dad was killed when he struck a deer with his car.

G: Circumstance.

L: How do you know that?

G: God knows all. Whenever one is seeking information such

as this, it is best to simply state, "Universal Presence, may we please interpret the tragic circumstances befalling this being of light here on earth. Amen."

Then may the answer be revealed. Let's take this for a test drive, shall we?

L: OK. My friend Kristy died from melanoma at age thirty-six. Beautiful girl. Beautiful soul. I miss her and think about her often.

G: And she of you as well.

L: Chosen circumstance or created? Dear God, may we please interpret her death accurately?

G: Circumstance.

L: Really? I would have said created based on how often she visited tanning beds and the fact that she lived in Florida and was in and out of the sun all the time.

G: Circumstances dictated that she leave the earthly plane early in order to know herself as mother of a fallen child.

L: But she died, not her daughter, so I don't understand what you mean by mother of a fallen child?

G: In order for Kristy's soul to evolve, she (as she was presenting herself in that particular body form) must know herself as a mother in heaven watching over her daughter as she seeks to grow and evolve upon earth. For Kristy is her daughter's spiritual angel along the path. Your brother is this for you currently.

L: So we don't just grow and evolve in body form?

G: Certainly not.

L: We also do this in spirit form?

G: The vastness of our universe is so expansive, so unlimited, that it would be impossible to inscribe upon each and every circumstance for which you may grow your soul. For it is upon all of you to ask, "Within which plane of existence am I currently, and how best may I achieve my soul's goals?"

L: And how may we do this?

G: Through mindful pursuits of quietude and contemplation.

L: So again, meditation?

G: Precisely.

L: This book is stranger and more fascinating than our last book. I think people are going to really start to wonder if I have lost my mind.

G: Here we shall say you have found your mind. Losing one's mind is not possible in spirit form.

L: No wonder I can't sleep at night. These conversations are exhausting and draining. My energy is zapped.

I took a few days off from writing to give my brain a break, and sure enough, I was bombarded with unicorns.

L: Thank you for my unicorns.

G: Do not thank us. Thank you. Simply in your awareness of these magnificent creatures, which we had inscribed upon together, you brought about more and more of them. This is universal law, that which is like unto itself is drawn. For whoever undertakes focused intentional awareness has the necessary tools for bringing forth more and more. Manifestation is the word we use for this wonderment.

L: I feel as though everyone is on the manifestation bandwagon right now. People are constantly posting about it, and mindset coaches are popping up everywhere.

G: Is this a bad thing?

L: No. It just feels as if it's something trendy rather than something people truly believe in.

G: Do you believe in the process?

L: I'm not really sure. I do, and I don't.

G: And why is that?

L: Because while I put my awareness on unicorns in this book (sort of accidentally) and they did show up for me in many ways (Facebook, posters, a commercial, a movie we were

watching, a girl's socks, and more), most people are trying to manifest money, including me, and that stuff never works (at least for me right now).

G: What about the hundred-dollar bills you saw?

L: What about them?

G: Your awareness was placed upon them, and did you not later on see someone giving them away?

L: I did, but when I tried to win the money I didn't.

G: And why do you think that is?

L: Well, it wasn't from lack of trying.

G: Well, there is your main problem.

L: The trying?

G: Perhaps we shall explain it this way so you know what is truth and what is of ego. (We are in control right now; of that you can be sure.) The main problem from which all humans suffer is *doubt*.

"I doubt I can win that money. I doubt that kid over there will call my name when I raise my hand to say I am here and wish to play a game."

Doubt is the ego's tool for stopping the flow of everything, be it money or machine guns.

L: Why do you keep making me write machine guns! I didn't

want too, but you made me write it again after I erased it, twice. So please explain.

G: Doubt is a fool's game no matter what the circumstances. Let us first take the notion of money. No one being upon your planet has ever been taught that there is enough for all in this vast multiplex of a universe. Yet, there is. This is spiritual fact.

"I doubt I can win the lottery," you would all say.

Yet, one need not win a lottery to be rich. Wealth is acquired in many, many ways in many, many places and through many, many channels. How do you bring about wealth for yourself and others? By not stopping the momentum. Universal law dictates that which is like unto itself is drawn. Like gravity: what goes up must come down. In what your healers have dictated as law of attraction, what goes out, must come back. Therefore, one must place your bets, so to speak, to even be in the game. Spend, spend, spend, we would say. You all would say save it for a rainy day. This is no action, and therefore, no reaction takes place.

L: I am finding this hard to write. What is stopping me here?

G: You are stopping yourself here. You are stopping the flow of information because your own doubt and worry are preventing you from inscribing what is the universal secret sauce. Spend and save. Spend and save.

L: I thought you said saving is not good?

G: We said no such thing. Here we shall explain the money-making secret for all of eternity. Make your mark by making a move. Act, and the world acts with you. React and save, and more will come through and to you. Save it. Spend it. Save it. Spend it. The cycle keeps going.

L: **What about those people who do spend money but don't give anything to charity or do charitable things? If you are spending on shoes and save for retirement will you get more? Or will you get more only if you spend it on others and not yourself? What are we saving it for? For ourselves? For others? I feel as though we need a lot better explanation here.**

G: And we will give it to you. First, we will say that those of a charitable nature are tithing (donating) monetarily, but not always are they charitable and gracious toward others. Yes, it is true that in the act of giving away, they are bringing forth more from themselves. This is not to say growth of soul will have occurred. The laws do not separate soul growth from spiritual acts or acts of ego. Therefore, it is quite literally possible to give, receive, and return and remain rich in dollars but be bankrupt in spirit. You do know many men of this stature, would you not say?

L: **I do, and there are plenty of women as well who I would place in that category.**

G: Precisely. For women are perfectly capable of the same.

L: **This is why the rich get richer?**

G: The rich get richer because they have tapped into a universal law, that which is like unto itself is drawn. We have used this phrase many times, and let us now break it down in simpler terms for anyone who is not understanding of its concepts. Money is a magnet. Unless and until you attract something to that magnet, nothing will attach itself back.

L: I get what you are saying, but I can definitely tell you it is easier said than done. Most people don't or won't give up what little they have, because they are afraid and doubting they will ever have more.

G: Fear and doubt; for you have just proven our point.

L: Well, how do we stop the fear and doubt when our pockets are so empty? If we give our last dollars away, we won't eat for days or weeks, or we would be kicked out of our apartments.

G: So what?

L: So what? Did you really just say so what? So what is that we could possibly starve or freeze to death, or worse. Ugh! Stop making me write "or worse"! I keep erasing it, and you make me rewrite it. Why do you keep doing that to me? What is worse than death?

G: A fate worse than death is anyone who doesn't seek for their truth.

"I am a child of God and the Universe. All roads have been paved for me. All moneys have been freed up so I may eat today or pay my bills."

L: Meaning, a fate worse than death is—

G: Not knowing who you truly are: a perfect child of the Universe capable of creating in and of the likeness of God, be it money or machine guns.

L: OK, here we are back to the machine guns. Out with it. Let's go here. What do you mean by that?

G: An ego's mind is capable of creating chaos in one's body temple as well as in any mind trapped in anguish or despair. The ego's tricks are many because it knows universal law as well.

L: I am feeling itchy right now and distracted, and I am writing words that do not seem right.

G: For where have you now placed your awareness?

L: On my itchy arm. Is this an ego's trick?

G: Precisely. This is how ego's irrational-mind thoughts work. Your awareness is upon the problem now.

L: Yes, and I keep having to scratch. So I am getting distracted from our conversation.

G: Precisely what the ego wants for you. Distract and deflect so that I may destroy machine gun fire. Bang. Bang. All your hopes and dreams are dead.

L: But you said "doubt" is the ego's tool of stopping anything, be it money or machine guns. So this doesn't seem to make sense, because the phrasing makes it seem as if the ego is stopping us from having money flow to us or guns flow to us (if that's what we so desire).

G: What we are saying is that—

L: I am doubting right now that you can answer this?

G: Yes.

L: My ego is stopping me from being answered.

G: And how may we fix this?

L: Dear God, may we please rightly interpret this information and release ego's distractions from my body and mind.

G: What is a machine gun for?

L: Shooting things at a rapid pace?

G: And what are our thoughts? How do they come to us?

L: At a rapid pace?

G: We have told you prior in our earlier book to not misinterpret words and phrasing. Therefore, it's always best to seek the answers within, which is precisely what you have done here. Machine gun fire is a metaphor for all of life's true moments. In every waking moment, you are thinking thoughts that kill the psyche and harm a soul's true nature of love. Abundance is your birthright. Stopping the flow of money is made possible whenever one who seeks rewards and riches harbors money for purposes of paying bills. Starting the flow of miracle-minded thoughts is stopped whenever one's ego places its flag upon the psyche. Thou art at war with guns blazing and marchers ready to return fire whenever fear, doubt, and worry enter the battlefield.

L: I'm sorry, but your phrasing still doesn't resonate with me. Again, you said, "Doubt is an ego's trick for stopping the flow, be it money or machine guns." Wouldn't the ego want to not stop the flow of machine gun thoughts?

G: Who said machine gun thoughts were bad ones? As we had just inscribed here with you, minds are thinking rapid fire, in constant motion, like a machine gun. Ego is meant to shut down rational thoughts, which erase all doubt. Ego stops the flow, be it money or rational-minded thought patterns.

L: I am still confused, though, because you said of machine gun thoughts that "in every waking moment, you are thinking thoughts that kill the psyche and harm a soul's true nature of love."

G: For this is not in reference to our rather strange explanation but instead to everyday ego thoughts, such as "I am not good enough" or "I am unworthy of joy and love."

L: I'm still confused. May you please accurately interpret this information?

"Machine gun fire is a metaphor for all of life's true moments. In every waking moment, you are thinking thoughts that kill the psyche and harm a soul's true nature of love."

So in this explanation, I assumed you meant they were bad thoughts.

G: A simple misunderstanding. Perhaps it would be best to separate the two sentences. Let us do that now.

L: "Machine gun fire is a metaphor for all of life's true moments."
Decipher that accurately please.

G: Rational thoughts are only what is true in this rationally based universal plane you are currently of body in.

L: Then you said, "In every waking moment, you are thinking thoughts that kill the psyche and harm a soul's true nature of love."
So the two phrases juxtaposed—

G: Is where the confusion arose.

L: So can we state this more clearly?

G: When in doubt, you may always ask for clarification. Whenever doubt is present, one may remind oneself that truth is precisely accurate only when and if one re-minds back with the maker, as we have done here to inscribe precisely the point. Doubting whether what was inscribed here was true led to an altercation in which you questioned the nature of the conversation and rightly asked for answers. Doubt is an ego's trick.

L: Well, why don't you just say it that way in the first place? Say, "Doubt is the ego's trick for stopping the flow, be it money or rational-minded thought patterns," rather than a word that obviously incited anger in me like "machine guns."

G: Too easy.

L: Too easy?

G: Too easy for one such as you, our inscriber. If we use unfamiliar words that seem irrational, then we are illustrating how doubt works. Your doubts about what you were hearing stopped the flow of machine gun fire—rational-minded thought patterns—and you got angry and frustrated and debated whether or not to erase all of this and start over.

L: I absolutely stared at the computer and was thinking about that.

G: And yet you did not. For you know enough now as a child of the Universe who is awake and aware that a great truth was about to be uncovered about doubt.

L: Doubt is what stops the flow of money, to go back to our original question?

G: Doubt makes it possible for ego's agenda to prevail.
    "You are a poor sucker," says the ego.
    In truth, you are rich in love, rich in finances, rich in rewards, and rich in romance. Yet you may only reap these riches and rewards when in giving. In giving shall you receive that which is already yours to begin with. *D-O-U-B-T.* Don't-Overthink-Unclutter-Brain's-Tricks.

L: That's pretty good.

G: We know.

L: So you are telling me you made me go through this whole thing just to prove a point?

G: Yes. Do you have any *doubt* now who is really running this show? Ego or God?

L: I have no doubt. Ego likes to come along for the ride sometimes, though.

G: And how shall we fix this?

L: "Dear God, please remove any and all words that are written from ego's perspective. Amen." Is there anything we wish to remove?

G: No.

L: I think when it comes to money, people want guarantees, and this is our biggest stumbling block. We cannot wrap our heads around the fact that if we spend our money, it will return to us. Especially if people are spending money on overpriced toys, cars, jewelry, shoes, etc.

G: What do the wealthy spend their money on?

L: All of those things. Yeah, but they have the money to do that. A girl making ten dollars an hour working retail cannot afford to spend her money unwisely. And, I see lots of people going into debt by spending, spending, spending.

G: What did we inscribe earlier is the cycle?

L: Spend and save. Spend and save.

G: Precisely. The cycle is repeated over and over, but spend,

spend, spend, spend is not a cycle. It's like throwing money into a trash can and rolling it down a hill. Place the money in the can, and roll it down the hill, but keep some in your pocket—now you have a way to make more by the simple fact that you kept it. Starting over again each and every time ensures the cycle will continue. Remember that everything in life is cyclical. Spend. Save. Spend. Save. Give. Receive. Return. Up. Down. Back. Forth. Nothing is just left without a right or down without an up. In order to give, you must receive. In order to spend, you must save, and vice versa.

"Don't put all your eggs in one basket." Where do you think this saying originated? Putting all the eggs in one basket leaves no room for more egg creations.

L: Yet again. I am just blown away by all of this. I really hope the people who read these books understand that I am not the one writing all of this. No way am I capable of writing this way so succinctly (and rapidly, I would add). It comes to me just like that.

G: You are all capable. We have said this before. You know the answers within. Deep within lie any and all answers. Amnesia of the soul makes it difficult to uncover these truths, which is why we unlock them only when we cocreate and see ourselves not as separate beings but as children of the whole—the creations of the Creator, who know all and see all just as I do. We write together. Never separately. From this material will come inspiration for others who will do the same. We wish they find you and reveal themselves to you, be it twenty years or twenty minutes from now.

L: So I should seek out Neale Donald Walsch, who wrote the

Conversations with God series to let him know about this book?

G: And what would be your stopping point?

L: Fear and doubt. Damn you, fear and doubt. Go away!

G: Damning them will not make them go away. Only by giving them back to the Creator and spirit within may they be healed. Whoever undertakes this practice consistently will find their needs and will met.

L: Well, my will is to release these financial fears holding me back right now. Is there a prayer here we could say together?

G: "Dear God, as we go about our day, may we remember in each and every moment that God is our source for all wealth and financial abundance. May all paths be illuminated through me and to me, which will lead me to financial security forevermore so that I may give, receive, and return always. Amen."

L: What shall we say in any given moment of fear or doubt or worry, be it personal or professional?

G: "Dear God, Creator of all life, may all sentient beings understand that fear is not necessary in any given moment. Please take these unnecessary irrational thoughts from my psyche and subconscious mind so that they may be returned to the nothing from which they came. Amen."

L: It's hard to let go of fears, though, because we live in a society filled with hate and crime.

G: Perceived crime. Perceived hate.

L: We see so much "perceived" crime and hate; I feel as if it's ingrained in our brains to go straight to fear mode in many situations, such as being in a parking lot or a gas station at night when it's dark out. How can we release these consistent and persistent attacks on our psyche by the irrational mind? OK, yet again, you just wrote that last part.

G: We did. We are merely trying to prove a point here—any and all moments of perceived crime and hate are, in fact, attacks by the irrational mind undertaking irrational thoughts, such as these: "I am not safe. I am scared. I am capable of being harmed."

God is not capable of harm or being harmed. Therefore, you are not capable of these either.

"I am safe. I am guided. I am Love," is all one needs to say to remind oneself of his or her dual nature.

You are a being being separate; but you are also a being of light. Therefore, those reminding themselves back with the Oneness are, in fact, safe in the arms of God and the Universe.

L: Is there a prayer we can say during moments of fear, such as when we come home late at night or are alone in our homes?

G: "I am safe. I am guided. I am Love."

Our answer remains the same. Remind yourself of your true nature, and you are healed instantaneously of irrational-mind (ego) thoughts.

L: Again, I think this is something that is easier said than done. Often times, our sense of security is damaged by acts of violence and other acts of theft and the like and by

seeing them in the news or on social media and then taking that in ourselves. How can we see these occurrences and not internalize them? Even knowing all of these universal concepts, I still want to lock my doors at night.

G: Then you should.

L: Why?

G: Unless and until all sentient beings of light living upon your planet are understanding universal principles of which we are speaking here now, they will be at the mercy of collective consciousness ideas of separation and enslavement. This includes any and all actions that negate the creative power within. Those who steal suffer from the illusion that they have needs that may not be met by outside sources; they do not understand that most needs, if not all, are prescribed upon by the universal energy system we are calling God here. For only in cocreation are asks answered.

L: I get this concept. I really do. So there is a part of me that says, "Well, I will not worry about the safety of my belongings when I am out and about, because I know I am safe, guided, and I am Love at my core." Yet, I am also a part of the collective consciousness, and it sounds as though I am unable to escape some of those collective thoughts. May I ask which is more powerful: our individual consciousness or the collective consciousness?

G: Neither is more powerful, for they work in tandem as one system of energy, which is how all manifestations arise. This is why it is always best to create together, never separately. For when we are in cocreation as mind, body, and spirit, we are at our best.

L: So give me an example of how that works. I wish to live in a safe community, town, city, state, country, and world. How would I go about this as both the collective consciousness and individual consciousness?

G: "Dear God, together may we create an experience where all in choir are understanding the nature of reality in which only love is real. Place in my presence those who see only safety, not those who alarm and disarm. Whenever one who sees irrational-minded manifestations enter my consciousness, may they be reminded through my own thoughts, words, and actions that they need never again be manipulated by ego's irrational-minded tricks. Rather, they are safe in the loving arms of God, Spirit, and the angels. Amen."

L: That's great, but most people are still living in the illusions of separation here. What is the best recourse for me when being with others who do perceive crime as possible in their experiences?

G: Remind yourself of who and what you are in each and every circumstance, and that is all one needs to do. Whenever you are in choir with others, you must consistently and persistently be mindful of ego's tricks. This is all one need do to remain safe, guided and with Love.

"I am safe. I am guided. I am Love." Again and again we will repeat this.

L: I am safe. I am guided. I am Love. It does feel good to say this. It brings—

G: Peace. Internal peace.

L: It does bring me peace for the instant that I say it.

G: When you say it consistently, then you will know peace consistently.

L: Thank you. I am grateful for these books.

G: You are welcome, and we are grateful for the time spent in cocreation. Our next topic shall be about the notion of gratitude. Good night and Amen.

Thank God

" **D**ear God, as we seek to inform our readers of the divine nature of our being, we shall be reminded that we are eternal beings capable of creating in and of the likeness of God. In our sharing shall we be grateful for all that has come to us, through us, and here now shall we forever commune with our inner wisdom and guides. Amen."

Laura: When we last left off, you said we would speak of gratitude in this next chapter. So what can you tell us about the importance of gratitude in our lives?

God: A grateful heart is a key component to all manifestations. In our gratitude, we are painting an important portrait of that which has occurred through our asking.

"I am grateful to God for all our bounty, and glory be to thee a new day from which to begin again. As we begin again, we are reminded that all of life is a magnificent gift, a portrait."

L: **That's twice you have used the word portrait and twice that I have wondered what you mean by that.**

G: As always, we are glad you asked. A portrait is a picture of truth.

L: **The truth about what?**

G: Of what is happening in the love-based world, which all souls are vibrating to and through.

L: **I don't understand at all what you mean here.**

G: What is a photograph?

L: **A picture of something.**

G: What is a painting?

L: **An artist's rendering of an image or thing using pigments.**

G: What is a portrait?

L: **A picture or painting of someone or something.**

G: What is the difference between a picture and a portrait?

L: **I have no clue. I would ask you that question. What is the difference?**

G: There is no difference. There is only subjective reasoning.

L: Meaning what?

G: Meaning what you see is not what I see. When I look at you, I am looking at a portrait, a perfect image of a perfect, all-knowing, all-loving being. When you see you, you are looking at a picture—an inaccurate portrayal of something through a lens. Looking through a lens will never be the same as a portrait through the lens of the eyes of God and the Universe.

L: What is your point here?

G: Our point is that in gratitude we are thanking the Universe for that which we have and that which we seek through our focused intention upon it.

"I am grateful for this next book we are cocreating. I seek to inform and enlighten all who have come here."

These are words of will. I will the Universe to allow this material to be released, and so shall it be. "I seek" is a declaration of that which is already a part of you. For you are never alone. You are never without all that you truly desire. There is no thing you are not. You are the Universe. Perfect and beautiful. Strong and kind. This is how I see you. Is this how you see yourself?

L: If I am being honest—

G: Oh, please do so.

L: There are days when I feel absolutely beautiful and, despite my age, still see the same girl in the mirror I did ten or fifteen years ago. And for that I am grateful. Then there are the days when I feel old and tired and somewhat sad and angry that I woke up so late in life. Oh, what beauty and magic I could

have created if I had known about the truths of the Universe twenty years ago. I would be unstoppable.

G: You are still unstoppable. You are kind and loving, beautiful and perfect. Those who seek perfection will see themselves as perfect once they know and understand all beings of love and light are magnificent, radiant manifestations of pure love.

L: Why can't we see that when we look in the mirror though? Why can't we look upon ourselves as beautiful creatures despite our outer appearance?

G: All of the all of you are hiding who it is you truly are. These are masks you wear, costumes if you will. They are not truth. Just as masks are hiding the person underneath, so too is the visage you look upon each day. The truth, which lies beneath the mask, is absolute magnificence. When you go to your mirror in the morning may you look at yourself and say, "I am a child of our Universe. Let the eyes that look upon me now see the truth of who I really am inside. I am a soul who lives eternally. My face and my body are but mere manifestations of what I am feeling on the inside."

L: What are you saying here?

G: We are saying how you view yourself is of ego. We have spoken about this in our last material. "Of ego" is the binding tissue that creates, from its standpoint, who it thinks you are from your thoughts, words, and actions and those of the consciousness of minds surrounding the bodies, which they have chosen at will.

L: I am not sure I am understanding here. May you please explain it in simpler details?

G: Thoughts. Words. Action. It has been established here and in other source material—

L: "Source material" as in books and CDs that were channeled through God/the Universe?

G: This is the only source of which we speak, yes.

L: I thought it was important to make this distinction so it was not misinterpreted.

G: What we are meaning to say is that all notions of one's mind-body-soul are at play here. This is to say, "As I see, so shall all see me as that which all wish me to be."

L: Meaning what?

G: Face value.

L: I am utterly lost here.

G: About face?

L: Yes, I am lost about the face!

G: We are joking with you here. We feel your frustration as you write, for this is not the conversation you were expecting here tonight. Therefore, we must ask you to repeat with us a prayer to release the channel and allow our words to flow more freely.

Here shall we say, "Dear God, it was not my intention to discuss issues of self-image or self-defacement. Here now may we return to our conversation and increase the volume so anyone here with us may understand universal truths and be more aware of Love's presence. Amen."

L: I think I am distracted because my neck is bothering me for some reason. May I ask what the reason is? I know it is something that is bothering me subconsciously.

G: It is all related to our conversation here. We shall show you now your issue. May you please close your eyes and listen quietly?

L: I heard, "Your problem is you." My problem is me? I guess I feel as if I am being a pain in the neck to other people because I am in the middle of promoting our first book.

G: You are worried, fearful, and so much more.

L: You know, I thought you were going to say it was because I got Botox the other day.

G: We know, but this is not your soul reason.

L: Sole or soul?

G: Soul. Release the fear of burdening those seeking enlightenment, and all notions of illness manifesting within your neck will thus then disappear.

L: How may I release the fear to God and the Universe?

G: "Dear God, my fearful notions of unkind and unloving behavior toward others by taking hard earned money from those who seek freedom from life's perceived tragedies are keeping me stuck in patterns of self-agitation. Let all paths be paved; let all monies be blessed. I am forever grateful for financial burdens being lifted. As we seek to enhance our soul shall we be paid handsomely so that all may be blessed by and to abundance. Amen."

L: I love all your prayers. They are so incredible.

G: Was that gratitude we just saw from you?

L: It was.

G: Bravo, dear Laura. Bravo. Your transformation is miraculous. You are almost ready to be that teacher you wish to be.

L: Almost? Why almost? What is the missing link?

G: Only missing pieces of the picture. The full story is in the portrait.

L: Oh, I like that, bringing it back to the original question. I am guessing what you mean is that we need to finish our entire conversation (in these *All* books) before I understand the complete and total magnitude of how this all works?

G: Precisely, for while you are remembering at warp speed now, you are still, in fact, remembering. Though you seek to inform others of our universal truths, we have yet to unlock many, many more ideas and anecdotes to wake you up fully and completely.

This is not to say that you may not continue to preach and teach, but here we shall remind you that whenever one is sent to or through you who seeks enrichment of soul, you must remind yourself to seek answers within and without.

L: May you clarify please your last statement, "You must remind yourself to seek answers within or without"? Why do I keep hearing, "The devil is on your back"?

G: There is an energy within the room that seeks to harm you.

L: What! Dear God, may we please release this negative energy back to the heavens.

G: Do you feel better?

L: Not really. But I followed the protocol being prescribed in these books by turning toward God immediately. I prayed for a result, and I am holding on to fear. That scared the crap out of me.
   "Dear God, together shall we release any and all negative energy from the room; may we bind minds and release all fear of future failures."
   Hey, wait a minute. You were toying with me, weren't you!

G: We were, yes. You see, "the devil on your back" is a statement of that which we were speaking on. To bind minds with one who comes seeking enlightenment, you must first remind yourself of who you truly are—pure spirit. Then and only then may a healing take hold for another. Earlier when you spoke with someone within your home, you were asked for an opinion on a medical issue. Once asked, you replied almost immediately, and yet you forgot the most important component in duality: that which is like unto itself is drawn. Upon your refusal to cocreate in that moment, you drew a negative ion. From this negative ion, you sensed an energy in the room (a.k.a. "the devil on your back").

L: You mean earlier when I heard what sounded like someone typing at my computer and I wondered if some spirit was in my room?

G: Yes, you believed with your own ears that an unknown entity perhaps had caused said noise.

L: I did. I truly did. Whoa, this is all so crazy.

G: For this is how the mind works. Illusions are created based on subconscious interactions. Had you known in your forgetting that you would deep-rootedly enact a negative result, you would have instantaneously turned back to Creator and declared your invitation to cocreate, and a new result may have come.

L: Why only may?

G: For you always have free will. Were you to have said the following prayer after the session, then a different result may have occurred through you and to you. "Dear God, I was not in my right mind when I answered a client's question earlier. Here may we release all negative, subconscious notions of betrayal by her and to her (or him). I ask for a healing for both client and clientele so that we may be healed together. Amen."

L: So what you are saying is that whenever we are with a soul or person who has come to us in asking, we need first turn

to God or Spirit (or whatever you wish to call the Universal Presence) and say—

G: Call upon.

L: Call upon the voice within in cocreation? And what shall we say?

G: "Dear Source of all beings and light, together shall we bring about a healing for our dear brother-sister who has lost their way in this earthly illusion. Let all of our minds join so we create a space where healing may begin to take hold. For all are reminded in our loving arms of the universe that they are never alone, not for a single second. We feel all feelings together; we speak, think, and act as one in all circumstances, and here shall we be one as well. Amen."

L: That is really good. These prayers floor me. Now what the heck were we talking about earlier? We really got lost on a tangent there.

G: Do you not see how it all relates?

L: No. We were speaking about self-image and then my neck problems and how to help others by making sure—

G: Mm-hmm.

L: We cocreate. Oh, right. This is how it all relates. Everything comes back to cocreation. Make no decisions on our own?

G: We wish that you go to bed after this, but yes. Make no

decisions on your own. When you look upon yourself, say, "Dear one, you are beautiful and perfect. We are perfect. Our divinity tells us so. May we never look upon ourselves again unless and until we see the beauty within. Amen."

L: Even when we look at ourselves in the mirror we have to remember our dual nature. Before we wrap this up here, may we please discuss this earlier statement, "As I see, so shall all see me as that which all wish me to be"?
Can you explain this to me please?

G: You see yourself as separate beings; therefore, you create for yourselves images of one another that serve an ego's agenda.

"She'd better not be prettier than me," or "I hope she doesn't look like her father or have his nose."

L: What are you saying here?

G: We are saying you are all at cause for the visage. Face value. What you value most, or least, is what you will see in another. That which is like unto itself is drawn; we will repeat this over and over again until you get it, you truly, truly get this. What you see is what you get. What you say is what you get. What you do is what you get. What you have is what you are.

L: Meaning?

G: What you have is all of the thoughts around you.

L: So you are saying the way we look is a direct reflection of the thoughts everyone is thinking of both themselves and those around them?

G: Yes, in a sense. You are a mirror upon their perceived inadequacies.

L: So if I don't feel beautiful about myself, my son is a direct reflection of that—

G: By being the polar opposite of that which you see in yourself. Think yourself beautiful, and then you will be beautiful, and those around you shall be as well. Think yourself ugly and that you have a face "only a mother could love," and then you will see ugly all around you. For one's expression is an expression of who they see themselves to be, be it ugly or glorious.

L: But I said when we started this conversation that somedays I feel beautiful and somedays I don't.

G: Thus you are proving a point we have just made here. What you see is what you get.

L: So because I see myself as both ugly and beautiful, I view others as such (as does most of the world).

G: Yes. You view others as such and create within body temples the need to deface that which you see yourself to be in service to the ego.

L: So I view my son as handsome because I feel both beautiful and ugly. What would happen if I viewed myself as only ugly?

G: Then may you create the opposite. A child of magnificent beauty may be seen in your estimation. "Beauty is in the eye of the beholder" is a perfect explanation for the systems at play here. All eyes look upon one another through the lens of ego and decide for themselves that which is beautiful and that which is "ugly." In our eyes, the eyes of the Universe, you are all beautiful, every single one of you. This and only this is what we see.

L: Well, damn. I must be Beyoncé to you.

G: You are all Beyoncés, Leonardos, Madonnas, and others whom you deem attractive on your planet. Do not mistake our gesture of love as a proclamation of adulation of a certain type of body or skin color. Our idea of beauty is much more than limited minds may ever inscribe here. You are perfect, each and everyone one of you. It would do you well to remember this as you go about each day, and as you look upon one another say, "I see beauty in all things. Amen."

L: We started here talking about gratitude. Let's go back to that please. From a spiritual perspective, why is it so important?

G: Not just from a spirit's perspective but from a human's as well. Should all be gracious and kind always?

L: Of course. But we are speaking in terms of the metaphysical reasons here.

G: Same reasons. An attitude of gratitude is stating a case for more manifestations of love, joy, happiness, or abundance, be it human or otherwise. All ego is cast aside whenever we declare our love to God and the Universe. Though some may not see it as such, this is very much their truth. In any moment of graciousness and thanksgiving, you are bringing forth more. I tell the Universe, "I am."

L: That's true. When we are grateful, we do use "I am."

G: "I am grateful for my blessings. I am full of wonder over what tomorrow will bring. I am so honored and blessed to share this material with you."

L: Thank you.

G: You're welcome. It feels good, does it not, to know you are appreciated?

L: Yes. It does.

G: We feel the same.

L: We don't appreciate God or the Universe?

G: Not often enough, no.

L: Yet, what happens if we don't show our appreciation and/ or gratitude?

G: What happens is often times you will feel alone and unloved, searching desperately for answers to life's great mysteries.

L: Like I was?

G: Precisely. An instantaneous prayer of supplication—"I am

grateful for all of my blessings. Though I don't have much right now, I know, dear Universe, more is coming. I stand in faith and know guidance is upon me. I listen with an intended ear and a grateful heart. Infuse me with your wisdom, dear Universe, so that I may lift up out of this dark depression. Amen."

L: I love that. I will listen with an intended ear and a grateful heart more often. What would be the wrong type of prayer?

G: Well, there are no wrong prayers, as in the asking, you are seeking; only unhealed prayers exist.

"My heart is broken. I am lost. My head is screaming. I am sick. My name is sullied. I am ruined."

L: People don't use the word sullied anymore. How about "My name is trashed"? Let's try to keep this somewhat modern day here.

G: Well, hello, ego.

L: What do you mean?

G: We mean that we will inscribe here from a space of love and admiration for one who undertakes this difficult task. Our words are your words, and although some of them seem old or unused in many decades, we are reminding all reading this material that all worlds are happening all at once. So our inscriber's vocabulary is more expansive than she/he knows.

L: You just called me she/he. Is that because—

G: You are all just one gender, as we have inscribed in our last book. This is how we see you all. The all of all of you. There is no separation between us.

L: Well, I apologize. I am grateful for this material and to be able to sit and accomplish such a miraculous feat.

G: We do not ask for apologies, only understanding. All sentient beings are capable of so much more than they know. Vocabulary is just one of those many, many miracles.

L: I could use a little miracle right now because I am dealing with a common illness—

G: Perceived illness.

L: Perceived illness that I get every so often where I get canker sores in my mouth. It's actually been a fairly long time since the last one, but can you give me any insight into what gives?

G: What gives is your lack of faith in what you are hearing. Here we shall reveal you have read and reread this material so many times that your familiarity is remarkable. Yet, in every way you are still doubting that that which you are hearing is not only true and accurate but coming from the otherworldly being of which you have inscribed here as God.

L: Yes. If I am being perfectly honest, though, every time I read this and our other book, I marvel at the feat we have accomplished here together. I still get tripped up in the notion that this can really all be happening, because it seems so absolutely, positively crazy and nuts. It's almost as if I am living in an alternate universe.

G: And, of course, you very much are; all of you are.

L: And all of this is a dream, a very strange trippy dream I am going to wake up from and go, "Oh, hey, you guys. I just had a dream where I wrote several books where I was talking to God, and God was answering me in the most elaborate, yet hauntingly accurate way."

G: Your point?

L: My point is that even though it sounds like something that should be a dream, I am very much aware that I am not in a dream state at all but rather completely awake sitting in my chair inside my home typing out a conversation I am hearing inside my head with what I am being told to describe as God yet am realizing is not really an accurate term in any way, shape, or form.

G: All of life is this great, grand illusion. You feel as if you are either sleeping and dreaming or awake and living. Yet in actuality, you are both sleeping and dreaming and awake and living. You are all things all at once. So though it feels as if you are wide awake (while sitting in your chair), you are also at the same time dreaming in some other realm.

L: What?

G: You are consistently amused, and we are always enjoying the reaction to our words.

L: So let me get this straight. One of the "mes" is in another

realm, in another incarnation, and is asleep right now dreaming about sitting in a chair writing a book with God?

G: Not with God per se, for you are not knowing with whom or what you are writing. Rather, you are dreaming of a circumstance where you are at cause.

L: At cause for what?

G: At cause for whatever fears are present.

L: So this other *me* is dreaming about writing a book as a way to wake herself—

G: Or himself up. Yes. Though said, *you* may have no idea this is possible nor any idea which manner of asking you should use to rightly interpret your dream.

L: Are you telling me that another *me* was actually the girl trying to give a speech who was interrupted by scaffolding being placed in front of her (as we discussed in our first book) in a dream I had?

G: Yes. Have we not told you of the nature of duality? For all things, for all souls. All experiences are happening at once. As one dreams, one wakes. As one wakes, one dreams.

L: So each of our incarnations has the yin and yang factor? Can multiple incarnations cross over one another?

G: Yes, insomuch as the waking and dreaming may not be in direct correlation always. It is quite possible to dream of one life tonight and another tomorrow. It is also possible to wake and sleep at the same time.

L: What do you mean by that?

G: One of the *yous* would be aware of the other just as you are doing so here.

L: Can we talk to our other *yous*?

G: Not in a waking state, no. In a dream state, absolutely.

L: I am intrigued and shocked, yet as always, it does make absolute, complete sense. Why would I think that? Why would I write that? Why is it now so easy to hear and type? The information is coming so rapidly now.

G: You are transformed, capable of cocreation at its highest form.

L: How many people can do this? I mean, sit down and type questions and hear the answers back immediately?

G: Millions upon millions are doing this all day every day, yet they do not realize it.

L: But of those who are capable and knowingly participating, why have very few shared their words with others?

G: Oh, there are many who have: Deepak, Oprah, Gabby, Marianne, and Eckhart (among others). Yet many others are not capable of concentration and enrichment toward others. For their audiences are and will be much smaller than yours. This is not to say all who are inscribers (of our healers) are not perfectly capable of such a feat; all who undertake this are. We are simply explaining that your background has made and will make your journey of accomplishment and achievement easier and vaster than the journeys of others.

L: My clairaudient gift has been awoken completely here for sure. Can we go back to my perceived illness issue, then, so we can wrap this all up for tonight and I can get some sleep? What is the problem with my mouth?

G: The problems with your mouth and dryness of your lips are in direct correlation to fears of speaking one's truth. For all whom you have told and have yet to tell may harshly judge these efforts here as unfathomable and insane.

L: Spot on, my friend, spot on. Wow you should be a doctor.

G: We are. Doctor God, MD.

L: I can't get over these fears, especially because even as I try to promote our first book, there are so many, many people living within the illusion. Half the time I am having to downplay the message just to get attention in the media. How many times in a day, in an hour, in a minute do I have to release the fears of what people will say back to Spirit until those fears disappear?

G: Fears run rampant. This is yet another term we have cocreated via inspired thought with other scribes. Whenever fears invade in any circumstance, they are instantaneously releasable. "May we please remove this thought from my mind." An asking as simple as this may be undertaken by all. All seeking to know themselves as Love or a divine being of light may undertake simple notions of healing until irrational thoughts have disappeared completely. Minute by minute, moment by moment. Catch and release. Catch the thought, and release it to the heavens. Repeat.

L: How long would it take?

G: It depends on how deeply rooted of a subconscious fear it may be. Money is a powerful magnet for fear. Love is a powerful connection for releasing fear. I love myself enough to know in any moment that all of us may be healed.

L: Money is tough because it isn't just our own individual issues, such as living in a house with a giant staircase, owning a firearm in a house filled with kids, or jumping a six-foot fence. You are writing these for me, aren't you?

G: Yes. Money is binding, as it's a commodity for all of the human race to obtain. Therefore, does it not make sense that releasing a fear in a world filled with poverty is near impossible?

L: Yes. It does, but it can't be impossible, right?

G: Nothing is impossible, but it is improbable to the like.

L: Meaning?

G: Anyone in lack is the like. Anyone perceiving themselves as empty and poor despite the magnitude of their current bank accounts are impoverished, be it monetarily or spiritually. Those seeking to enrich their lives both monetarily and spiritually must undertake daily focused prayer and intention to release the notions of lack and scarcity ingrained upon society.

"I am rich," not "I am poor." Or "I am capable of creating wealth and abundance in my experience, and I release any and all notions of poverty to our maker. We are an abundant society with never-ending resources around and available to the all of us. Never shall we remain in lack again. Amen."

L: So it's not enough to pray individually, because this is such a worldwide issue? We need to remind ourselves there is enough for all of us, not just ourselves.

G: Precisely. "I am a money magnet. I attract wealth and prosperity for all. All for one. One for all."

L: Yet again we got off on another tangent. We were talking about my mouth issues. Can we find a proper prayer here?

G: We may. But first, we shall say to all who are listening or reading or perhaps watching one day that no one of you thinks a thought alone. Therefore, it is always right in any asking to remind yourselves of this.

"We are so grateful for all our gifts. As we seek to enhance our fortune, so shall we enhance the lives and fortunes of others. What goes around comes around, always. Amen."

L: Great. A fantastic prayer that I will be repeating moment by moment until I release that deeply embedded fear, and I will remind myself of this in other prayers. Now, about that one for my mouth.

G: "Dear God, as we seek to release this material, together shall we create an experience whereby I may speak universal principles for all seeking to know themselves as the Oneness as well. Though I may not know which path to take toward enlightening other beings, I allow that the Universal Presence guide me toward those who are seekers. My words shall be perfect and true here and in other materials. I shall speak of myself and my connection back to the Oneness as gently and truthful as possible, and never shall I address this material as crazy or irrational again. Here now may I know the truth: that we are all one, and whatever has been inscribed upon here and in other source material is divine and accurate. Amen."

L: I realized today after talking to some friends that some people really, really don't like the word prayer. I was one of those people. Yet, I also now know it works. What's a good way to explain it to someone who has a hard time praying?

G: Focused intention. Your way of describing it earlier to our healer (at your gym) was perfection. "Focused awareness." This also is an accurate and wonderful term. You are focusing your awareness on that which you are releasing back to us.

L: Can we talk about channeling for a second? How am I doing this? How is it possible for me to sit at a computer and start typing questions and have the words be spoken back to me instantly in my head with no lag time with every word being perfectly placed and within context? This is remarkable, and yet I still question these concepts on the regular. I can imagine if this is hard for the person who is writing this book (a.k.a. me), how hard living these truths must be for someone who is just starting his or her spiritual journey.

G: Where there is proof, there is magic.

L: Yes, but if the proof is minimal and we see no manifestations in our lives rather quickly, then we dismiss it as new age nonsense. This is why so many people do not believe.

G: Those who do not believe are simply living in a space of unawareness. Though you are very well aware of Love's presence in and around your life, you are also aware of that which you feel you are lacking in any given moment. You feel as if you are in the unemployment line yet have no concept of future endeavors. You cannot see it. Therefore, you cannot be it. This is true manifestation at its finest. That which I cannot see is that which I cannot be.

L: But how is that manifestation? Wouldn't manifestation be bringing forth those things that we are wanting and/or desiring?

G: All that you are wanting is all that you are keeping away. In your desire are you telling the Universe, "This is what I already possess in spirit."

L: But wanting and desiring seem to be the same concept, at least to me (and I would imagine to many others, if not most).

G: Here we shall break it down into its pure intention.
    Want—I need this to make me happy.
    Desire—I already am happy; therefore, I need nothing other than what benefits my soul's purpose.

L: So our desires come from our souls, which is why we desire them in the first place?

G: Precisely.

L: And our wants or needs come from the ego?

G: Yes. Wanting a thing is an ego's trick for keeping all stuck in cyclical patterns of pity.

"I am angry and bitter. That person is rich while I am poor. That girl is pretty while I am ugly or unlikeable. I want more money. I want fame and all manners of intense adulation. See me! For if I am not loved and adored by strangers, why, then I must be nobody special. I am not special. I am not unique. I am ordinary. I am sad and unhappy, and if only I could get more money, more adulation, why, then I would be happy."

Yet what would happen were people to attain those things they are wanting?

L: They might be happy for a little while, but then anger or resentment or jealousies may return, and then they are right back where they started.

G: They are back to where they began—feeling unhappy, unloved, uncared for, and alone. This is no way to live. This is "death" in its truest form. This is bankruptcy: a form of moral telepathy that reminds people of their untrue nature rather than their truest nature of divine love.

L: Moral telepathy?

G: Believing you are one thing when you are actually another.

L: So believing we are not good enough—unlikable or unlovable rather than divine beings of love and light. Seeing into and projecting the future for ourselves as something we are not.

G: Precisely accurate. Yes. Being angry about a thing that has not happened yet is ego's way of imprisoning its captor. Torture not the mind by revealing a false image of that which you think yourself to be rather than that which you already are.

L: And desires, to go back to that, come from the soul? Do ego and soul ever clash in this? Like if I am wanting another child but also desiring one; is this a clash?

G: This is not a clash but rather a confluence of energy whereby both systems of energy are merging.

L: So ego and soul can sometimes get along?

G: Yes, in many ways they are a perfect marriage. However, like in most marriage unions, they are often split on ideas of the heart. An ego may want a child to love as its own as a means to bring love (which it feels it is lacking) into its own life. In the meantime, a soul may desire a child for purposes of reconvening with an equal or opposite partnership.

L: So ego wants to fulfill a lack of love, and soul wants to use it as a tool to grow and evolve itself further?

G: Extremely accurate.

L: I thought that ego and soul were always at odds, though?

G: Not always, no. Ego is the driving force in most manifestations, if not all. Money, fame, houses, cars, and other items of ownership that seek to enhance an ego's self-image. However, when a desire of the soul is at play, well, then ego and soul are a dynamic duo capable of superhero-like manifestations.

L: Such as?

G: Children, artwork, opportunities for advancement in career pursuits, achieving one's dream of acting or getting a movie role, making a touchdown, harvesting a bounty. Anything that moves a soul forward while at the same time allowing others to experience a joy as well.

L: Can an ego manifest on its own?

G: Ego is acutely capable in connection or conjunction with the laws of the universe whenever flow is enacted—give money, get money. Though this is also at play in radical measures.

L: You mean like if someone decided to rob a bank to get money?

G: Precisely yes, or take another's life in pursuit of radical-minded objectives, as your Taliban and other theology rebels do.

L: But don't manifestations arise mainly from a soul's and ego's merging agendas, so to speak?

G: Manifestations arise whenever soul and ego are in cahoots, yes. To both want and desire means both ego and soul are in choir. To want without desire is in many ways an impossibility; rather, it is an ego's deceit. I want this only because I have a partner, child, friend, parent, or coworker wanting it, and therefore, it is upon me to give to them what it is they are wanting though it is not within my soul's purpose currently of this incarnation.

L: I both want and desire more children. Though my ego is now telling me I am too old and that too much time has passed, my soul is ready to reconvene with these other souls.

G: Ego has lost control, so to speak. No more are you wanting a child to fill a void, but rather, you are desiring the children you feel around you at all times. Does this not make sense? Resonate within your soul?

L: Can we only desire something without ego being involved and still manifest it?

G: Yes, without question. This is where all desires are more quickly released. For this is when an ego has lost control and, therefore, is incapable of destroying one's manifestation capabilities. Let us look at money as an example here for you. "Where am I holding on to fear?" we shall ask here first. Let us look upon it now. Close your eyes and listen.

L: I heard, "You can't get there from here."

G: And from whom would you say that is coming?

L: The ego?

G: No, think again.

L: I heard, "Where does money come from?"

G: And where would you say money comes from?

L: From God, the Universe, Spirit supplying it at will?

G: And will you allow money into your life?

L: I would if I could.

G: When you can, you will.

L: Why can't I? What's stopping the flow?

G: You are stopping the flow. Have a think on it again.

I closed my eyes.

L: I see or hear nothing. OK, let's say a prayer here. "Dear God, may we release any and all manifestations of fear energy, which stop the flow of information from coming to me right now."

I closed my eyes again.

L: I heard, "You are God."

G: And what does that mean to you?

L: It means I must be crazy for thinking that. No. It means that we are all capable of bringing into our lives—

G: That which already is yours, yours for the asking. This is how true manifestations come true. In the asking, you are looking upon that which has already occurred in your lifetimes. You are rich. You are not poor. You are a dreamer. You are that which you dream of in all manners of sleep. Awake and arise and declare, "I am the dreamer, and all that is available to me is mine for the taking. For I have had it in all planes of my existence. Somewhere within this vast universe and cosmos exists the *me* I long to be. So shall I see it. So shall I be it. Amen."

L: We really do go in circles, don't we?

G: For this is by design. All matters are cyclical, as all matters are of the same system of energy—Love vs. Fear. This is Spiritual Principle 101. Therefore, like any good reminder of truth (a.k.a. teacher), one must return to the same concepts over and over until the inscriber is confident in the material. Questions will continue to arise as well of a cyclical nature until she has "come to Jesus" and reflects those principles consistently, belovedly.

L: So can we wrap up this particular conversation here? What is the best way to manifest money?

G: Be more. Have more.

L: Meaning?

G: Be abundance. Have abundance. We have touched on this many a time before. You must be what it is you say you are wanting to be. All matters of money are on a want-need-desire basis. You want it to make life easier. You need it to live on. You desire it as such that it already exists for all who come seeking riches upon your planet (in their current incarnations). Enlightened masters have no need for material possessions though they are understanding of money as a commodity of giving, getting, and receiving upon your planet. They take what they need, so to speak. Most upon your planet, however, are not enlightened masters or anything close, so they are praying to a system of energy (a.k.a. money) that establishes a life of grandeur.

L: Money makes life easier. I don't think it is the be-all and end-all to have it; it is just that joy is more easily accessible without struggle.

G: A brilliant interpretation of money's necessity. Joy is more easily accessible without struggle. This is why we, as the All of Everything, are here always to remind you of joy on the regular. Those in lack tend to miss these magic moments.

L: Tell me about magic moments. What things should we be enjoying on the regular?

G: A glorious sunset. The crisp fall air. The smell of the rain. The laughter of children. The bark of a dog. The march of a band. The rainbow in the sky. The waves of the ocean. The light of a tunnel. The bounce of a ball. All these and so many more are moments of enjoyment that are missed and ignored by so many within your planetary system in favor of technology and other online pursuits.

L: And when we are missing them is how we keep our manifestations at bay?

G: Precisely accurate. Yes. Focus on the lack, see more lack. Focus on the joy, see more joy.

L: So then is this the answer for how to manifest money? Focus on joy, laughter, etc.?

G: Be at peace with where you are and who you are.

L: What about the spend and save and the give, get, receive notions. Aren't they at play here?

G: Yes, you did not let us finish. Focus on the lack, see more lack. Focus on joy, see more joy. Save a little, spend a lot. Give a little. Give a lot. Keep the energy flowing (money, love, exercise, abundance), and more will flow.

L: This is why if we don't exercise, we get flabby?

G: Yes. This is also why when partaking in unhealthy narcotics or alcoholic substances a system of energy flows, which allows for manifestations of addictions. Cut off the flow; cut the cord, so to speak.

L: I think that's easier said than done with an addiction.

G: Addictions are flow manifestations. That is all.

L: Yes, but what of someone who goes to rehab and gets clean but then within months or years takes it back up.

G: Well, then the flow is flaring up again until one is reminded of their true beingness through transformation or tragedy.

L: How did we go from talking about money to talking about addictions?

G: Same system: energy. Everything is energy. Momentum keeps the flow going. Spend, save. Spend, save. Light up, drink up. Sober up, start again.

L: I am not sure I want to get into a whole conversation about addiction. Though I get what you are saying, I think we should just leave it at that. Let's just keep this to a conversation about money. In order to keep the flow going, you have to keep the flow going (i.e., be willing to part with money so more money may flow to you). Give, get, receive and that whole concept.

G: Be willing. Yes. A willingness to be that which you say you wish to be is a magic formula for manifestation. Most upon your planet are not willing to part with their dollars.

"For this is all I have to give," most would argue.

And we would say, "Give what you have so that more may be received."

Our will is your will, but only those who are willing will succeed.

L: So just by placing our awareness upon money won't bring it to us. Like the unicorns. I see them everywhere; like, every day since we talked about them. But no money has come to me though it's always in my awareness.

G: Precisely why you are keeping it away. Your awareness upon the lack of money is what keeps it away. You are not currently lacking unicorns, are you?

L: Ha ha. No!

G: You are laughing, but this is, my dear, the secret to all manifestations. Become unaware of a lack, be willing to move the energy, and you can and will be a master of manifesting.

L: Does this apply to babies?

G: Same principal.

L: License plates?

G: When you are unaware, do they arise out of your willingness to see our signs and messages?

L: Yes.

G: And what happens when you are asking for them and are aware you have not seen them in a while?

L: I don't see them.

G: And what happens when you are unaware of them?

L: I see them.

G: Aha.

L: Aha.

G: That which you feel you are lacking is that which you will keep at bay.

L: So I should go out and start spending my money?

G: Spend wisely? Yes. Spend frivolously? No. Though it is not wrong to spend frivolously on ego pursuits, such as cars, motorcycles, large mansions, and other high-dollar things, it is not spiritually enlightening or sound to do so.

L: Well, how would we know the difference between spending wisely and frivolously?

G: You will know the difference when you ask yourself the following questions: "Do I want this, or do I desire this? Do I need this to survive?"

L: Let's take a pair of shoes as an example. Some Christian Louboutins. Do I want these, or do I desire these? Want. Do I need these to survive? No. OK, so that's a frivolous purchase.

G: Let us take the example of a toy for your son.

L: Do I want this or desire this? I desire for my child to spend time at play rather than on his iPad. Do I need this to survive? Well, it does make it easier for me to get stuff done around the house when he is busy.

G: What about a new car if you are driving a beaten up old car?

L: Do I want this or desire this? I desire a safe car for my

family. Do I need it to survive? Yes. It helps us get around places, to get me to work and my children to school.

G: One more. Food.

L: Do I want this or desire this? I want to eat healthy food. I desire to feel good on the inside. So I guess that one is a little of both. Do I need it to survive? Yes.

G: Do you see how this works?

L: I think so, yes.

G: "Put your money where your mouth is."
   In spiritual form this means to ask so that you may receive an answer on soul's true desires.

L: I desire to stop dwelling upon lack and to move on from this subject forevermore. I am willing to see this differently.
   "Dear God, may we please move on from this subject. Release any and all notions of fear we may be holding on to as it relates to finances. Together we shall remove all notions of lack from our subconscious minds and be willing to keep the energy flowing as a means for more manifestations of money. Amen."

A few days went by, and as usual, I was struggling with these concepts.

L: A lot has happened in the last few days, and not all of it's good.

G: Let us begin, then, where we left off: praying to your money system.

L: Yes, we prayed, and I was great for a couple of days, but then—*wham!*—all those same cyclical thoughts and feelings came back to the surface. This might actually be impossible, at least for me (and I would imagine for some others). I get why people fall right back into their same old patterns after reading spiritual books and material. We are creatures of bad habits.

G: A precisely accurate representation through wording here. You are creatures of bad habits. Never have you been able to not dwell upon the lack; therefore, you have been unable to gain abundance of any kind, be it spiritual, financial, or wellness. Focusing upon lack ensures more of the lack.

L: Well, so many things keep happening that are reminding me of that which I am lacking. I am lacking a job (currently). I am lacking my youth (currently). I am lacking a commitment by anyone to release our book (currently).

G: Why do you feel you have been guided to write in this particular manner with the word "currently" in parentheses after each statement of lack?

L: Because each of these things is only temporary? A temporary state of being—

G: In lack. A temporary state of being in lack. Don't you know after all this time that all roads have been paved, all errors have been corrected, and all financial means have been made available?

L: No.

G: Well, this is the very problem from which you all are (currently) suffering. And what may I ask you is a current?

L: A steady stream?

G: A steady stream, or flow, that takes you down the river of life. Don't let your current issue stop the flow. One door closes; another one opens. An obstacle arises—shall we go around it, through it, or over it?

L: All the above.

G: Yes. Very good. All those things and more; go beyond it. For what lies beyond is far better than what stood before you.

L: So that message today about the shopping cart outside Whole Foods was for me? When I pulled into a parking space, there was a cart in the way. I thought about going through it or moving it but instead went beyond that space and found a new, better one.

G: A new, better something is always waiting around the corner for those whose beliefs match with their trust. No does not necessarily mean this is a stopping point. For you are the chooser of your point. You may move forward, move aside, or move backward. You choose. You decide. Your will is our will. Life's daily challenges are ever present. For this is your "human nature," as you all would deem it. This is to say that whoever seeks enlightenment within your planetary system will, in fact, be faced with road blocks and obstacles for purposes of growing and evolving beyond all circumstances, all of which have value.

L: What could I be asking myself when challenges do arise?

G: How am I meant to grow from this challenge? What needs to grow in me in order to transform this experience so I may move beyond it? Ask yourself now. Go on. Then tell us what you have heard.

L: I heard, "Move out of a space of being and into a place of knowing." I thought we were meant to be; to just "be that which you say we want to be." That was the ending of our last book.

G: We do ask you to be that which you say you wish to be. What is at issue here is the knowing you can actually be it. This is where all humans get hung up on their philosophies of being. I am being. I am knowing. I am.

L: Back to the I am.

G: Yes, for this is purposeful because you are not yet knowing yourself to be a teacher of spiritual truths. You are knowing yourself capable of being that which you say you want to be but are not knowing you are this.

"I am a speaker. I am a healer. I am a seeker of inner truths. I am speaking to God and all of his constituents and cocreators upon Mother Earth and in planetary systems outside of the realm of our current world's view scope of knowledge. I am."

L: "I am capable" should be replaced with just "I am"?

G: Yes. For this would have a marked improvement upon your inner world view of yourself. "I am capable" is acceptable unless and until you are knowing and being that which you say you want to be. Once you are there, you will not have a need for capability, for you will have knowing-ability—an even more powerful positioning of inner truths.

L: I would imagine based on having written half of our second book together that there is a plan here where readers of these books would need to read these sequentially and take part in the entire series before getting to that inner knowing?

G: Those who read these materials and others are not necessarily partaking in all of it. Those who do deem to remind themselves of spiritual wisdom will find value in your words for purposes of resurrection and introduction to somewhat radical, albeit similar, concepts previously discussed in other books and materials. Yes, they would do well to continue with our dialogue from start to finish. Though it will never be finished from a spiritual standpoint, at some point we will wrap up this particular series of books and materials.

L: I am grateful for this interview and grateful for our time together. Although I know some of our questions and answers can be repetitive, I would imagine this is by design, especially for those who are coming to these concepts for the very first time. I have been studying for the past two years, and clearly, I am still just a puppy in training.

G: You are all still puppies in training in relation to your entire earth's journey within our planetary system of checks and balances.

L: I thought there was no judgement. So how can we have checks and balances?

G: Yin and yang. Up. Down. Left. Right. Back and forth.

L: Oh, you meant this not as some grander story or new thought; you simply meant it as the yin and yang theory of evolution.

G: Exactly. A job well done. You are learning more and more quickly—when it doubt, we can help you out!

L: Funny. You changed your voice in my head to—

G: To that of a cheerleader, which is precisely who and what we are. Go, Laura!

6 Guns

"*Dear God, as our country continues to struggle through tragic events and circumstance of gun violence on a repeat daily cycle, may we share universal truths with all who seek to transform our world's view, both inner and outer. May all who come to read these words see their value and our intention to enlighten and inform, never to harm. Amen.*"

Laura: I am really shaken up yet again. I mean, it's been barely a month since our last mass shooting in America in Las Vegas (in August 2017) at a country music festival. Now another shooting just happened in a church (November 2017) of all places, and twenty-six people were killed. Parents. Children. Siblings. Friends. Why? Why does this keep happening? First of all, what is our main problem, and then can we get to the fact that this occurred inside of a house of worship of all places? You have really got some explaining to do here. Otherwise, I might throw this book and the last one in the garbage can.

God: First of all, may we say here you will do no such thing as to dismiss all that we have written here and in our prior material on account of one unmistakable tragedy occurring in a sacred place of counsel and quietude.

L: A place of counsel and quietude? What do you mean by that?

G: For this is precisely what it is. A holy temple of contemplation and reflection upon the values a society deems accurate.

L: What are you saying here?

G: We are saying that places of worship like these are solely made for those seeking impunity from God's wrath, which we have told you there is none.

L: I am sorry your honor, but I am going to have to disagree wholeheartedly with your summation.

G: Go on. We are listening.

L: I know plenty of people who attend church or synagogue and other places of worship for a sense of community or who go to pray to God because they believe in a kind and loving God and not in one who condemns and damns all sinners to hell. I know from my perspective, even as someone who is not associated with one religion, that I would feel safe walking into a church or a temple and think it is a haven. Isn't this why many churches leave their doors open to all who seek shelter?

G: May we remind you of the guns you have witnessed upon security officers outside of a holy place of worship just this past weekend? Your awareness was perhaps placed upon these for a reason. For this is what is happening all over your world, not just in the country in which you are currently living. There is, in fact, a real sense of insecurity sweeping your nation. Upon all citizens of your earth is an alarming unconscious fear of being gunned down by another being who they would say had questionable morals and ethics.

L: Questionable? How about morally bankrupt, broken, lost, and mentally ill. I hate to break it to you, but most of these attacks are carried out by mentally deranged individuals who—

G: Have lost their ways. They have simply found an outlet for their anger and venom upon those they believed to have wronged or harmed them.

L: You have not said one word to make any of this better or to satisfy—

G: Your ego.

L: No, my anger.

G: Thus you have just proven our point. Anger comes from the ego and the notion of separation, but continue please.

L: We just keep creating the same experience over and over again, and in every passing circumstance it gets worse and worse and worse. A school, a concert, a movie theater, a

shopping mall, a place of worship, a bike/walking path. What's next for goodness sake? I think we have run out of places to shock and dismay. It's as if we have been desensitized to it all. No one seems to care anymore. Nothing is changing. No one in politics will stand up and stop this madness and get these gun laws changed. Nor will the pharmaceutical industry admit its antipsychotic or antidepressant drugs are at issue here as well. The fact is that every single issue comes down to greed and money and power by corporations and conglomerates.

G: Are you done?

L: Yes, I think so.

G: Then here we shall say you are not wrong in your above summation. For all of these are human aspects at play within the current illusional nature of gun violence. No man, woman, or child need have the right to bear arms ever in any civilized society.

L: But we are not living in a civilized society; not yet anyway.

G: This is, shall we say, the crux of your current illusion problem of violent capabilities of mass shooters. Within your very uncivilized society is the notion that harm can come to any of its inhabitants. Therefore, a right to bear arms was established upon your nation by its founding fathers as a means to protect its citizens.

L: But our world has evolved and changed, shouldn't our laws change? This is what most moral and ethical people would

believe, I would hope. Yet nothing, literally nothing, has changed. We just go back to our lives and sit back and wait for another tragedy while our lawmakers cower in the corner too afraid to make a move. I'm sorry, but this is a messed-up country and world we live in currently. Oh, back to that—currently. You wrote that part.

G: Yes. We did. Currently are you living in a governing system that seeks profit above all else; a system established long ago by your fathers' fathers and their fathers' fathers.

L: Right. That is not at question here. The laws are old and in keeping with older traditions. What is at question here is how to fix a broken system, which, as it currently stands, is killing our citizens in a multitude of ways, be it with gun violence or pharmaceutical drugs.

G: Drugs are not your problem. People are your problem. The conscious unhealed mind, which thinks and behaves in a manner that serves the ego, is at war.

L: I'm sorry, but I am not going to let you get away from the original topic, which is why a holy place, such as a church, with a group of people who worshipped God was a target. If all of those in the congregation prayed that day to stop the violence in the instant it was happening (and I would imagine they did), then this renders all that we have written in this book and the last one as pretty useless. Prayer did not stop a gunman from murdering our brothers and sisters. God did not heed their prayers or warnings. Yet again, you are writing my words for me. "God did not heed their prayers or warnings." What warnings would you mean here?

G: Warnings of impending doom placed upon an altar of the mind. We remind you that all who seek to know God must know that God does not pick or choose whom to harm or whom to help as a means of punishment. This is not God's wrath or vengeance, nor is it God's will or corruption.

L: What do you mean corruption?

G: Placing a gunman in a house of worship is not a punishment or a proclamation of prejudicial indictments of any one religion (such as is being batted about all over the internet currently).

L: Is it really? I had no idea.

G: Yes. Your "internet trolls," as you have deemed them, have made very clear their beliefs of wrong and right from their egos' main standpoints.

L: Can you just very simply explain why a church became the next target in the gun violence debate please?

G: For this is a great way of phrasing this.

L: Why?

G: Gun battles are waged whenever ones who seek profit are at war with ones who seek religious freedom or impunity from ego's irrational thinking: "I am in power. You are my pawn. I am the puppet master. You are the puppet." A church (in many regions of the world) is nothing more than a house of worship and profit for the puppeteers. This is not to say those who come to know God within its four walls are not coming from a space of love, for many of them are; rather, we are saying one cannot seek God and find spiritual wisdom in any place that seeks profits over pride. Your world works the way it does because mass consciousness cannot and will not move beyond this issue of gun impunity. Fear not the wrath of the people; fear more the wrath of government and its constitution, a constitution we have told you needs redrafting from a new space of awareness. By the people, for the people—not by the lawyer, by the governor, by the congress. You vote upon a presidential candidate. Why can you not vote upon the ratification of a new bill of rights in which all Americans are afforded equal rights for all, no matter what ethnic makeup or gender each has chosen for this current incarnation. No man or woman or child need go hungry. No man, woman, or child need go without shelter, comfort, love, or commitment to healthcare for all. All beings upon your earthly planet are entitled to the same privileges of all other members, be they rich or poor and downtrodden—for all are equal under God. For this is what is stated in your Declaration of Independence, is it not?

L: It is—not in those exact words but a similar sentiment that we are all equal.

G: So why is it not followed to the letter? For all are equal under God. Who do you think wrote this doctrine, inspired its very wording?

L: You did.

G: We did. We all did. Ego's mind changed its core concept to reflect a concept that "all *men* are equal," but the inspired notion that each and every citizen living upon Mother Earth is of God (the energy of the Universe) came from the all of us—which is you, me, and we.

L: Again, I am tracking with you here, but somewhere along the way I am going to be teaching a seminar, and inevitably someone is going to ask me about why children were murdered inside a church or school, and those answers will not suffice. People want definitive answers here, not the same old "mass consciousness" argument.

G: This is not an argument. It is fact. Here we will say that anyone seeking to know God doesn't know God, if they are under the impression that God can stop said attacks and atrocities. God can no more stop them than you can unless and until all eyes look upon the actions of the few who do the most harm and state a case for no guns.

L: No guns at all.

G: No guns at all is impractical in your current world's view as it stands. This is not to say one day civilization may have no need for them at all (as is the case in many civilized societies), but this is not how the systems of earth currently operate, and so we would say that until it becomes civilized, guns must remain only with your military and law enforcement officers. From this notion we will never stray. You may ask a hundred times over, and we will state this a hundred ways over: guns need remain only with the military and officers of the law.

L: But why can't God stop these attacks?

G: We know you know this answer, but we will indulge one last time so all may be clear in the answer. Gun violence, insolence, desperate acts of betrayal, berating one another, attacking ourselves, our communities, our churches, and our outdoor venues of amusements, violent acts of a sexual nature, wars, and weather atrocities are born of out fear, fear-minded notions of harm and betrayal, scarcity, ungodliness, and unloving acts of denial of the presence of a supreme being (which you call God)—these all come from thoughts that serve an ego mind and not your true nature. These are the leading causes of cancer. Let your commercials and marketing materials reflect this divine truth: nothing happens to you—the all of you—that is not through you, and therefore, stopping these fear-minded events is upon all minds responsible for them. Think a new thought, and have a new experience—together. For this is why God, as you deem to call our energy system, cannot and will not stop any such attacks. It is violating the free will of the thinkers to think how it is they want to think. Want to think a new thought and create a new idea? Then think as I (God, the Universe, Source) think. See our worlds for all of their beauty and magic, and replace all insane thoughts together as a collective consciousness. There can be no other way for your earthly world to stay in high vibration unless and until the all of the all of you agree upon one thing: we are all Gods and, therefore, incapable of creating anything of harm or despair.

L: Well, thank you. I want so much for people to understand this concept, but I can also understand why they don't. When you are affected by a tragedy or see a tragedy, then you are—

G: Infected.

L: Infected?

G: For then you are trapped within ego's clutches; all minds bind together upon your planet, Earth, and (save for those who are enlightened enough to see them for the illusions they are) believe within their cores that they are capable of suffering tragedies and travesties of a same or similar magnitude. For this is how you infect an entire society with a disease, such as your eighteenth-century plague, polio, HIV, and other infectious diseases, like those we had inscribed upon earlier.

L: How do we stop this individually for those who are enlightened, awake, or awakening? What can we say to help to release the idea from our egos or subconscious minds that has been implanted by the mass consciousness?

G: "As I look upon these tragic circumstances brought on by irrational choices, may I see through the illusion into the heart of the matter; may I see that all manners of existence upon this planet have created conditions whereby tragedies and travesties may occur. For these circumstances are not true but rather madness. For this is not real but quite unreal. Though I send my love and light to these beings of energy vibrating at a lower level currently, I also know that I am capable of so much more. As I think a thought from my highest self, I see a bright light of energy, which sweeps me into the momentum of love. In every moment may I feel Love's presence within. Amen."

7

Soulcieties

*"*D*ear God, let all of us come together now to share inner truths and reveal illusions of separation to the All of the All who come seeking this reinformation. Amen."*

Laura: It's been only about four months since we began this journey of writing, and yet again, for the third time, my child is sick. It's on repeat cycle. And by the way, I have done all you told me in the earlier portion of this book. We have prayed. We have used empowering phrases. I have used subconscious techniques.

God: And what was the result?

L: I felt as though it worked, for the most part. It started out as a terrible persistent cough and high fever. We prayed for him to feel better. He set his intentions to stop coughing. He talked to the cough and told it to go away. I even did some energy healing techniques to break up the energy around his chest. This morning he woke up and still had a fever but

virtually no cough. I was prepared to run him to the doctor, but he seemed pretty good all day except for the fever.

G: A fever is a fighter of bodily invaders.

L: I typically don't give any type of fever reducer medicine unless he is really cranky. Yesterday he was having a rough time, so I did give him a couple of doses.

G: And today?

L: I let the fever do its work. What would be a proper prayer to help since all minds are connected, and you say we can subconsciously affect our children's minds?

G: "Dear child," you will say to him before you head to sleep, "you are loved and guided by an unseen spirit, which walks with you wherever you go. Release all fear-based thoughts leading to a condition of cold and cough symptoms. Remind yourself as you sleep that you are a child of the Universe. All is well. You are whole. You are perfect. You are Love. Amen."

L: Why do we go in circles in this material? Why can't I get to a place of total enlightenment where I have no need to worry, doubt, or fear anything? Struggle. Enlightenment is a daily struggle, at least for me. It's as if I cannot get out of my own way here. Do you understand?

G: We understand it is hard for most, if not all, seeking reconnection back to Source Energy.

L: Why? Why is it so hard? Just when I think I have gotten

all of this, something spins me backward yet again, like my sick kid. A setback, a challenge occurs, and then I feel as if I am right back where I started. I don't get why this is so hard. Honestly, it's not until I go back and read over our first book and what we have written here that I am reminded very starkly that there is no way I wrote all of that, and therefore, this must be truth. I do that, and then I am able to begin again, start over and replace the fear with knowing.

G: For have we ever said one time this would be an easy conversation or comfortable endeavor?

L: No. I guess not.

G: All who come to read these pages, these words, will face similar struggles and setbacks. For this is the nature of humanity, to pander to one's ego mind. This is why it is imperative in each and every moment of irrational-minded thinking that one doesn't let ego thoughts rule the roost. One must return in each and every instant to godlike, egoless thinking and say, "These thoughts I do not wish to have. Take them away now and forever."

L: Yes, I understand that concept after having written it so many times before, but I feel as though when I do that, eventually after a day or so the fearful thoughts return. The "I am not good enough. I am not worthy. I am not smart enough. No one will like me. No one will read this. No one will care. People will make fun of me for this" thoughts return.

G: And why do you care so much about all of these things right now?

L: This is my ego talking?

G: Thinking. This is your ego thinking for you. For you are all perfect creatures in the eyes of God and the Universe, capable of creating in and of the likeness of the Creator.

L: I know. I know. I have heard this all before, so why can't I stay in that knowing? Why, after all this time, am I still doing the same things over and over and over again and again and again? I am so frustrated with myself and with the process. It works, and then it doesn't work.

G: Excellent; we are now getting to the heart of the matter.

L: What matter?

G: You are divine beings, all of you, but what you are not being is consistent. We have spoken of this before, and again we will remind those seeking enlightenment here—you must be consistent in your daily quietness, a daily dose of spiritual wisdom. An apple a day keeps the doctor away. Here we will say a prayer a day keeps the ego away. Daily prayer, quiet meditation, intention, and goal setting—these are the tools of a spiritual guide and warrior. Be here now. Practice, in any given moment of fear, anger, reservation, frustration, or passionate denial of Love's presence in a body, a new thought or a focused intention to cocreate with all of the Universe. Then and only then may a new pattern of energy emerge.

L: How much time? How long does it take to get this—to really get this and actually do it, stay in daily, consistent practice until our thoughts are aligned perfectly with God's?

G: Forever.

L: Forever?

G: Yes, forever. For this is how all worlds are designed to operate. A system of energy whereby the all of the all of us continue to grow and evolve until said time that we understand ourselves to be that which we say we are wanting to be—perfect, whole, and complete. For this is a never-ending process of creation. Over and over and over again all of you must make this choice—consistently. Consistency—this is the secret ingredient for a life lived fully and completely as a body. Consistent, daily practice is paramount for all good, ungodly thoughts to be redeemed. Think of it like the checkout stand at your local mall. "I would like to buy this shirt; here is my credit card."

Swipe the card. Spend the money. Take the shirt home. Unwrap the shirt. Wear the shirt on a fun night out. Launder the shirt. Place it in the drawer or closet and forget about it. A shirt sits waiting to be taken out again. Many times, we have a favorite shirt we take out over and over again. This makes us happy because we desire to look a certain way. Many times, though, we have shirts waiting around to be discovered again. These are your unhealed thoughts—you must take them out again and again until you are done with them and ready to donate or throw them away. Replace "shirt" for "thoughts." Do you see where I am going with what I am sure at first seemed nonsensical?

L: Is this in reference to hidden thoughts? They sit around in our subconscious closets waiting to be taken out and used?

G: Yes. Hidden thoughts, both good and bad. I am smart—good. I am sad—bad. What happens if we take out a shirt we later decide we don't like?

L: We get rid of it.

G: Precisely. Get rid of the shirts (thoughts) you don't like. Keep the ones you do.

L: I would imagine our subconscious closets are full of hidden skeletons that we have long forgotten about or wish to keep buried.

G: Is it not possible you have buried these for a reason?

L: Like our ego buried them on purpose?

G: Yes, to keep you stuck in the closet.

L: My goodness. I can imagine if I am struggling with all of this, how hard coming out of ego's clutches must be for those who have some really tragic circumstances in their lives. I mean, my life has been difficult and filled with loss and grief but nothing compared to some others.

G: The heavier the burdens, the harder the process.

L: Is this why this has been so hard for me? As a reminder to me that those who are just starting the process will have an incredible, uphill battle and that it's not upon me to judge where they are in the process?

G: Rather, we would say it is upon you to help those who come seeking and only those willingly seeking; and understand their struggles and strife are necessary for their evolvement as souls.

Therefore, one shall never judge the process or the length of time it takes someone to grow and evolve.

L: Is all of this purposeful—all the ups and downs I have been struggling with throughout the writing process—to help me understand how to help others? To remind everyone who is reading or listening to this that change only happens when we stay consistent with our practice of removing ego thoughts?

G: Yes. Every action and reaction here and in the pages of your other book has been a purposeful cocreation by and through you to help grow and evolve the soul.

L: Well, good. So here is a story, then, to discuss. I am going to be brutally honest here about something because I want people who read this book to know that as human beings, none of us are perfect. We are all seeking enlightenment, we are, however, programmed from a young age to be something other than we are, which is pure spirit.

G: We are listening and ready to receive.

L: Today I went to a kid's birthday party with a group of strangers with whom I felt I had nothing in common. I felt like a complete outsider. I pretty much sat there being a judging Judy and openly annoyed by my circumstances, which is not the behavior a spiritually enlightened person should be exemplifying. Yet, as hard as I tried, I could not muster up the energy to make conversation. I am not even sure there is a question here, just an observation that perhaps we are inherently taught to be judgmental of those who do not speak our language or who are not in our socioeconomic class. What could I have done in that situation to be more godlike, to let my soul flag fly?

G: You need *do* nothing at all. You need only *be* who it is you say you wish to be. Bless a stranger.

L: I would imagine you mean that I could have said a silent blessing to each and every one of them?

G: Yes, to bless a stranger is to say, "I see you. I feel your struggles, your sorrows. Though we are of different levels in our search for enlightenment, I am here for you in spirit as needed."

L: This would have been better than just sitting there like a bump on a log not talking?

G: Yes.

L: I felt bad about my reaction to the situation.

G: Feeling bad and doing bad are two very different enemies. For when we feel bad, we activate our knowing of wrong-minded ideals. When we do bad, we are coming from a place of anger and strife.

L: So the fact that I knew I was being kind of a heel was a sign that I was at least aware of my behavior?

G: Yes, and, therefore, able to change it.

L: Thank you. Then that was an excellent circumstance for me to be in so I can do better next time.

G: And so we shall begin again.

L: Something has been on my mind for a while now. In our last book, you told me that in other civilizations they are not as violent as we are. I keep thinking about it, so I know I am meant to ask it.

"It is no different than the spears and knives your ancestors used. To kill or be killed is how you have all related to one another since the dawn of time and space on your earth. In other worlds, it is not like this. Only humans so far are, and have been, capable of the destruction of one another. There is another way, a way to peacefully coexist together as a nation, as a society, as a world."[4]

Yet I have recently read in someone else's book that other beings have been or are also as violent as humans can be. So which is the truth? Perhaps I am misinterpreting the words, and I wish to be reinformed here.

G: The truth is that humans are capable of the destruction of one another while in more civilized soulsocieties—

L: Did you just coin a term?

G: Why, I believe we did. In more civilized soulsocieties, it is agreed upon that to terminate another being's life is an unacceptable act unless agreed upon by both parties. This is not to say those who perpetrate violent acts are not incapable of destruction; we are simply saying no being may act upon rage or anger in a manner that terminates a "life."

L: So planet Earth right now is the only place where we kill each other intentionally?

G: Right now, yes. Perhaps we shall explain—in other worlds, bodily functions are very different from those of your own, which is why this possibility exists. Suffice it to say there are other planes of existence where war, violence, and other demonstrations of anger, deceit, or betrayal occur but in a much different way from your own current understandings. All beings upon earth would need to agree to this "termination agreement" prior for a circumstance such as this to exist upon your planet.

L: So these other beings upon other planes and planets agree before incarnating there that under no circumstance can they kill another being, no matter how angry or crazy they get unless it was put into place prior?

G: Yes, free will is always at play here though most have chosen to stay within the confines of the agreed-upon collective.

L: On no other planet do they kill each other willingly?

G: Not currently, no.

L: Why do you say it as "not currently"?

G: There are no absolutes. A multitude of possibilities exist upon all planets and places dependent upon all thoughts, words, and actions of both the individual consciousness and the collective consciousness for each plane of existence. Therefore, we shall never speak in a manner that dictates or pre-dictates outcomes. As it currently stands, there are no planes or places where beings kill other beings except upon your planet, unless it has been agreed upon consciously in both parties' agreements. So the information as inscribed prior is accurate at the time of this questioning.

L: So we pretty much are the worst. Great. Humans suck.

G: Being human is divine as is being other types of life-forms. It is upon only your planet where beings are currently in a state of not being. They are, rather, in a state of doing.

L: Funny. I have been thinking about this a lot today.

G: There are no coincidences. We are with you always. Therefore, our words are your words. Our thoughts are your thoughts. You are now being more than you are doing. For you have always been one who is more capable than most of being. Most upon your earthly plane find no good reason to spend time alone in quietude or contemplation. For there are so many things to be doing they would say. Do less. Be more. This is how all beings upon your planet should live. Do what makes you happy and brings you joy, but also be who it is you say you wish to be. Be with yourself, and the more you do this, the more you will be able to move into the knowing of who you truly are and what your soul's truest purpose is.

I took a trip out to California to visit friends and treated myself to a week at high-end hotels rather than sleep on friends' couches as I normally might do.

L: Today is the day after Thanksgiving, and I feel as though it has been a powerful time in my life. I am finally moving past the financial fears and actually practicing what is being preached here. I decided to spend money on hotel rooms for

the week even though I have no money coming and no full-time job. I simply asked myself in every moment, "Is this who I want to be? Do I want to be someone who fears spending money?" No. "Do I want to be someone who couch surfs because I can't afford something different?" No. "Do I want to be someone who stays in nice hotels and enjoys life?" Yes. So I spent the money and continue trying to move out of a space of fear and into a space of knowing, knowing I am abundant and that more will flow to me and through me.

G: You are growing and evolving experientially more and more. And what would you say is the difference for you now?

L: I change my thought patterns. I change my words. I change my energetic vibrations. I spend time with those who raise me up, not those who bring me down. I disconnect from social media and television more and more. I remind myself in as many moments as possible that I am a perfect child of the Universe. I have become more consistent with my practice and most importantly my understanding of these principles.

G: You are now ready to teach. You are remembering at a wonderful pace though you still have so much to learn, and from here on out our words may shock you. However, we will tell you that whenever you are feeling fear or doubt or worry, you must instantaneously ask for answers so that we may speak spiritual truths with no boundaries and no need to filter out messages of hope and wonder in favor of messages that will be more to your liking. You must get rid of your ego in all circumstances and serve the higher self.

L: I am trying. I feel at peace with all of this. I understand it. I believe it. I accept it. I know there will be days and times

of struggle, as I know all of us have experienced, but I will continue to stay in daily practice as much as possible until I am constant and consistent with all of it.

G: There will be bad days. For this is the nature of being human (and other culture-forms as well). The more one consistently practices, the more one is capable of moving up the soul growth ladder. Pray an instant, stay an instant. Remember this always so in times of need whenever irrational thoughts arise, you consistently remind yourself of Love's presence and go within for help. Seek within, for this is where all good answers reside. We are grateful for this time spent in cocreation and are grateful for these questions, of which you still have many. For many will arise as the days and weeks go by.

L: One of my questions is this—why do we forget all of this spiritual knowledge? Why can't we be born with this? Why do we have "amnesia of the soul," as you have called it?

G: You are born with this knowledge. So the question is not wholly accurate. "Why can't we remember sooner?" would be a more accurate phrasing here.

L: Then let's change the question. Why can't we remember sooner?

G: You are here to grow and evolve yourself through experiences of opposite polarities. It is, therefore, nonsensical to return or incarnate as a body and already know this.

L: Why?

G: Then you will already know rather than experience. Does

this make sense? You are meant to experience all things, and so if you were to return already knowing certain things, why, then how would you experience them fully without judgement and condemnation if they were not done to your liking or favor?

L: I guess I can understand that. We are meant to experience things in order to—

G: Grow and evolve through them. Yes. You do understand, and for this we are very grateful. We are so much more than one can imagine in this and other lifetimes, and so we will explain certain new concepts to you now.

L: Are the things that happened in each lifetime specific to that lifetime?

G: Yes. All lifetimes are happening simultaneous, and in each one you are growing and evolving through various circumstances, and so you are not the exact same thing in every lifetime. Lightning does not strike twice, nor do the same two experiences—unless a free will choice has been made, which is always possible but minutely, as most feel a calling to do something.

L: So this is why some people become certain things? Doctors, lawyers, painters, poets, actors, singers, therapists, etc.?

G: Yes. You all would deem it a "calling"; we would deem it a purposeful creation chosen by and for you to evolve further and beyond other experiential circumstances.

L: But why?

G: To grow and evolve from a place of pure being. You cannot be that which you say you wish to be unless you forget who it is you wish to be. What is the point of being something you have already been if you remember you have already been it? Why be a poet if you have already been this somewhere else? Why be a painter if you know how masterpieces are created? Why be anything at all if you know already how to be it.

L: I think I am lost.

G: I was lost but now am found again in the loving arms of the Universe. This dialogue is purposeful in explaining that in order to know who you are, you must forget who you have been.

L: And who have I been?

G: You have already been everything. So in this lifetime you must forget who you have been so that you may *be* it.

L: I still don't get it. If I have been a thought leader and healer in other lifetimes, as you have stated in our first book, then why would I want to be that again? I have already experienced that somewhere else.

G: Experiences, albeit equal in name, are quite different in nature. As a thought leader or healer in prior existences, circumstances for you were much, much different and complicated. For you had no reason to believe in any of this. A thought leader (as you were previously) understood no such notion of a Universal Presence, only a theology of God. Therefore, as a thought leader you were speaking in terms of a benevolent being. You believed at your core the God you were speaking of was good and decent and kind toward all. This is the word of God you shared. As a healer in prior incarnations, you believed primarily in the modality of medicine, or rather the medicinal properties of plants and shrubs. So these experiences were quite different in nature. We would add here that you got to where you currently are (in this case, a healer and teacher of spiritual principle upon your planet, Earth) by growing and evolving the soul further and further. We remind you that there are other planes and places, and you have not always been a thought leader or healer upon planet Earth, which explains also why or how you have been something similar. Are you understanding this more now, my dear?

L: Yes and no, and I still largely feel as if we haven't gotten to the core reason why we are given amnesia of the soul before incarnating.

G: This has been chosen, not given. The all of the all of you have chosen to do this for the reason that we have previously inscribed—in order to know yourselves as The All of Everything, you must then experience it for yourselves in any and all lifetimes. Remembering who and what you are will keep you stuck and unable to grow and evolve beyond who and what you are, which is Love. In order to know you are Love, you must first experience the absence of love, and in order to experience this, you must control circumstances of equal and opposite polarity. The only way to know love is to know fear, and if you do not know fear, you will not know love. So you return to a body or similar forms in order to experience fear so that you may know love. To know love, you must know love through any and all circumstances that have been created upon your planet and others. This is why you may live hundreds upon thousands upon millions of lifetimes in order to grow and evolve through any and all experiences until you know what you are, which is pure love. When you know love and only love, then you will have grown and evolved by all experiential circumstances, and then you may return to the kingdom righteously.

L: We forget who we are in order to remember who we are?

G: Exactly.

L: Why does it take so long? Why do we need so many lifetimes to do this?

G: Because at the core of your beingness is the opportunity to do this, and so most, if not all, decide to remember who they are by forgetting who they are.

L: Does anyone who remembers who they are come here to earth without amnesia? Are there people walking around knowingly being here?

G: Not as body, no. However, there are ascended masters capable of disembodying and embodying at will who walk among you at all times. These are your "miracle" workers, of whom many have spoken in this lifetime, and others you do not remember currently. Once you are returned to the kingdom (based upon your thoughts, words, and actions), you are reminded back to the Oneness whereby all simultaneous lives will be revealed unto you. Once this has occurred, one may then decide upon another incarnation in present form or various other forms in order to grow and evolve beyond one's last incarnation. This is how all beings of light are at choice in their circumstances.

L: You have stated over and over that we are never alone, that

we always have helpers, and there are teachers here to remind us of who and what we are. Why don't you give us the amnesia and leave us to our own devices to figure it all out? Why wake us up (if we are meant to forget who we are) to learn and remember who we are?

G: For this would cause mass chaos upon your planet and in other places that are not currently knowing and understanding there is a source from which all emanate. There are many places that know this consciously and still seek to separate from the Oneness in order to grow and evolve. There are more, however, who choose to forget in order to remember, as we have said here. There is no good reason we can see to not remind those back to the Oneness once a choice has been made to separate. We are wanting you to know love in any and all circumstances. This is how we guide you. This is why we guide you. Would a parent leave a child behind in a dark room and allow it to fend for itself among knives, guns, terrifying animals, or other children it did not know?

L: Of course not.

G: So too would we never do this. As the separation was created, so too were circumstances that were born out of fear. None upon your planet are left to their own devices or to fend for themselves, so to speak, because that would be cruel and unusual punishment, unless and until fear is wiped out.

L: Is ego something we have in all body forms in this current universe?

G: Yes and no. Yes, ego exists in other planes and places but not in all. There are many places where egos have been cast aside, and most are living within the illusion consciously.

L: Why would they do that? How would they do that?

G: They do this by way of right-minded thinking in all circumstances. They know within their souls that they are meant to experience all circumstances through the eyes and lens of love, and so they do consciously, as it makes for a much easier life journey.

L: But you just said that we are here to learn opposite polarities. So why would they only choose to learn within the lens of love if there is not fear. What is that teaching them, then, or how is that evolving them further if they only know love?

G: Highly evolved beings, such as these, are knowing only love in any and all circumstances; but this is not to say that they are not at cause for their circumstances. They are still under the illusion of separation but are consciously creating in every moment as a body form and are, therefore, at choice to view all circumstances from a standpoint of love and not fear. Their souls do know the truth and will give them what it is they are desiring, which is to know themselves as beings who see only love in all circumstances.

L: Are we capable of doing that as humans?

G: Yes, but most don't, as you know. Even you as you move into mastery are understanding that circumstances can be difficult and distracting. So you choose unwillingly (via the ego) to dwell in and upon fear.

L: I would love to stop doing this.

G: So stop doing this, and start being. Beingness—this is your truest nature. You are humans *being* not humans *doing*. Remember this as you go about your days and nights. Beingness reminds you that you are in fact a soul being a human, not a human being a soul.

L: Can I, can we live as humans on earth and learn through the lens of love always?

G: Absolutely. You are doing this now mostly, are you not?

L: I'm trying, but it's admittedly hard.

G: When you are consistently doing this task of learning through the lens of love and not fear, then you too will be a master of evolvement.

L: So we can be highly evolved beings on this planet?

G: Yes. There are many, and you are one of these, and though you are not yet clear on your path, you will be.

L: As humans, are family members always at the same level of soul growth? Do we incarnate with others who are similar to where we currently stand in our experiential journeys?

G: Yes and no. Yes, you are at similar awareness states. No, you are not evolving at the same levels always. Remember, each spirit is responsible for his or her own thoughts, words, and actions. So all beings upon planet Earth are individualizing their own journeys as well. One might feel as if a family member is behind him or her, but in actuality the family member is right on time in his or her placement of personal soul growth. Do not judge a familial relation by ego's tricks. Families are created whenever pre-incarnation choices have been made to grow and evolve together. One's choices are never to be questioned, only to be expressed by and through one another.

L: Earlier we talked about those who come here with Down syndrome. I would imagine when this happens within a family that it has been chosen—

G: By all parties involved, yes.

L: Why would a soul wish to do this if it knows that its mind may not be able to bring itself out of this circumstance?

G: Again, you are focusing upon this being a sentence, not a blessing. In order to understand all aspects of love consciousness, one must know what it feels like to feel love in all circumstances as body. As soul, this is, of course, your true nature. It is only when you are "of body" that often times you are capable of being unloving and unkind. Those who have chosen this circumstance are understanding of their choices, and they certainly know what it will entail; and yet they still willingly make this choice. Often this is a final stop along the way to mastery. For this is why we have said these wonderful beings are highly evolved souls. This does not mean that when they are of body they may not fall back into cyclical patterns of abuse and fear, for when you are of body you have forgotten all that you already know and must be consistently reminded through acts of love.

L: Can we remind them?

G: Absolutely. Consistently reminding them of who and what they really are will have a marked improvement toward their growth of soul as a body. "You are pure love" is all one needs to say whenever convening with these wonderful beings of light. Seeing them and thinking of them this way as well is part of the process of realignment back to Source.

L: You have alluded to this many times here and perhaps even in *The All of Everything*. Is there more than one universe? Some scientists and physicists believe we live in a multiverse.

G: Yes. We have been waiting patiently for this conversation with the all of you, and we feel as if you are the perfect conduit for this conversation now with the all of us.

L: Really? I just got goosebumps.

G: There is no shortage of ways we have tried to remind your scientists, physicists, and mathematicians of cosmology. Yet not many, save for Stephen Hawking, have grasped truly this vastly intricate multiplex from which we all come.

L: How many other universes exist then?

G: A multitude of universes exist.

L: Is there a God in each of these other universes?

G: No, there is only a universal energy system from which all emanate; that which you are calling God or Source.

L: Are we also part of these other universes?

G: Yes. When you are finished in one universe moving through all of your lifetimes, then you will move to another one. All thoughts, words, and actions will be wiped clean, so to speak, and you will begin again as spirit and soul seek to evolve through new and intricate cosmology.

L: Honestly, I am not even sure what questions to ask here. This is mind boggling to take in.

G: Is it? Or does it resonate within one's soul structure, however minute it may be?

L: A little bit, yes. I guess it kind of makes sense. I would imagine there are many things we will all learn when we return to spirit form.

G: Many, many things, and most of them would shock you in your current physical form. It is, therefore, advisable to "know before you go."

L: Seriously?

G: We are joking here with you, a culture reference to your TV commercials but no less accurate in terms of knowledge of other universal planes and places of which there are many.

L: What, then, is the next step in our evolutionary process?

G: To move beyond each and every circumstance in your current lifetimes so you may step out of this universe and into an entirely new one.

L: Does our soul come with us to the next universe?

G: Yes, of course. Soul is eternal, as I am eternal.

L: In each of these universes, is there an entirely new God?

G: There is no such thing as a God in any and all universes, only energy from which all emanate. God, as we have said, is the name chosen by much of your planet to name this energy system and give it context. Your question needs resolving within the context of energy. There is one overall universal energy system from which all emanate. In any and all circumstances, you are able to remind back to this one system.

L: We don't leave behind that energy and become something completely different?

G: No. It is all just energy moved by thought.

L: Do all the universes operate on a love vs. fear basis?

G: Not necessarily. Within each, an entirely new "operating system" exists—much like a computer has multiple systems—though love is the driving force in all; fear may not be the polarity, which is its opposite reaction.

L: So once we move up the soul ladder and are capable of

moving to another universe, what happens? Do our soul families come with us?

G: Some of them, yes. Some of them, no. Not until they too have moved up the soul growth ladder are they ready to move on to other universes.

L: In these other universes there is a whole different collective consciousness?

G: We are all of a collective nature, and therefore, there is only one overall collective, which splits itself between universes at all times. So a part of the consciousness remains with one while another is somewhere else. In the end, all minds join as one as part of the evolutionary process, remembering that we are one giant being of energy and light split into an infinite number of parts. And although there is only one energy system, it splits itself in much the same way as the collective consciousness.

L: Kind of like home base in a baseball game?

G: Yes! An excellent reference here—home base. We like this terminology very much. Bravo. We must explain that while you are a part of first, second, and third base, within each base lies a completely different system; but each base is still part of home base and the game. We remind you there is no such thing as God, only a theology of God made manifest by and through man and other beings upon your current universe. There is, however, only one energy, and this is why God is not with you in all universes. In other places and planes, the word "God" does not exist, and therefore, it is possible to not take God with you into these systems of energy. We are not ready to speak of these other beings and planes you would find within these other universes just yet, but suffice it to say there is an energetic system that is unique to each one, and it all emanates from the same source—a.k.a. home base.

L: I think I am going to drive to the beach and bury my head in the sand. This is so crazy to me.

G: Is it crazy, or is it truth? Why do you think a man such as Stephen Hawking existed on Earth? His knowledge of the cosmos was vast, and frankly (though many dismiss his musings as insane and most do not believe it and call it nonsense) it was quite close in accuracy.

L: Why was such a brilliant man locked in a wheelchair? Was this perhaps a chosen circumstance?

G: Perhaps he chose his path for a reason, which we cannot judge. His teachings would be so much less interesting had they perhaps not come from a man locked in a wheelchair. Would fewer people have paid attention had he not become famous for his circumstances as well?

L: True. Can you give me some idea of what happens in these other universes?

G: We are not yet ready to discuss this at all.

L: Why?

G: Because limited minds would have no true grasp of said concepts, as there is no wording that would suffice for this. These ideas go beyond what you all are capable of comprehending within your current lifetimes' incarnations.

L: Because we can't conceive of it, we can't understand it?

G: It is not that you cannot conceive of the notion of there being other universes, for many do understand this possibility. It is simply not possible to explain any and all circumstances from which to grow and evolve one's soul within your current understanding or language. It simply does not exist, the language needed to explain this, be it English, Spanish, or Swahili. Words in your universe are vastly different from others within the cosmos.

L: I guess I am just confused. So after we finish with our lifetimes in this universe and have grown and evolved our soul here, what happens?

G: Then you will move on to other universes as we have stated earlier. Your soul will go with you, but your energetic presence will stay behind.

L: Like an imprint? Our energy lingers?

G: Yes. This is why when moving into a new home or work space, you must clear the energy of the rooms or spacing. The energy remains unless and until you remove it.

L: Why wouldn't we remove the energy from the universe once we are ready to move to another one?

G: Because you are all things at once. You are in all universes.

You are in all things. You are of all things. You are me. You are you. You are we. You are up and down, left and right, back and forth. You are all things. No matter where you are, you are always there no matter what.

L: So we are everywhere always?

G: Yes, this is what we have been trying to tell you for two books now. There is nowhere you are not. There is no one you are not. You are the universe and the cosmos. You are other undiscovered and undetected places and planes. You are Source. We are all Source Energy split into an infinite number of parts and places, souls and bodies, grass or trees. Everything is energy. Everything living and breathing. Alive or dead. Near or far. This is it. This is the secret of all secrets. You are the pages of this book but also the entire book.

L: Is this why my document just split into six pages? In six months of writing this has never happened.

G: Yes. We did this to prove a point. A point that you will now make over and over until others begin to understand this truth of the universe. You are all one.

L: I get this. I truly get and understand this now. I could quit while I am ahead, but I still have so many questions. They seem to arise daily.

G: And this is very much by design. We are pointing you always toward new and complex understandings via various modalities of unlearning.

L: If we are all one—one mind, one energy, one collective consciousness—why then do we each split ourselves into individual consciousness? Why do we even have a soul, and why do we come into individual bodies?

G: Try to keep up here because this will truly shock you. There are bodies with a shared consciousness and soul.

L: To be honest I am not that shocked at this point by anything. We have seen this here on earth with conjoined twins.

G: Yes, these beings share a body but not a soul and consciousness. They are separate minds and think individually (from a body standpoint). What we are speaking of are beings upon other places and planes who consciously choose to share a body, mind, and soul (without knowing they have done this within the incarnation).

L: Why would the souls join forces like this?

G: Because there are an infinite number of ways to experience the divineness of your being, and this is just one in a multitude of ways we choose to do this.

L: But you are not answering my larger question of why. Why does Source Energy split itself in the way it does all over the place?

G: To experience itself exponentially in all matters of existence. To know everything. To be everything. To feel everything. To say everything. There are literally infinite ways of being, and to do this as one giant whole would be impossible. It does, however, become possible when all of matter splits itself into the All of Everything.

This is why we say we are all of one mind. We are experiencing the all of everything through commune with everyone and everything.

L: Then why do we experience so many lifetimes as individual souls?

G: Because no one experience is exactly the same, just as no snowflake is the same. We have said this before, to you and others. There are an infinite number of experiences to be and have, and this is why the energy splits itself infinitely—to experience itself exponentially, blissfully.

L: I guess I can understand that, but why, then, does everything exist simultaneously? Why do things not happen linearly?

G: Because, my dear, there is no time and space (this happens only within the illusion of separation), and therefore, things are not linear; they just are. Things are happening, always. They never did not happen. They just happen. It's like one giant computer filled with music and games, books and videos, apps and Word documents, which, when you bought the computer, already existed on the hard drive. It was all already there, and you are just there to enjoy it, to play with it, to watch it, to create with it, to be frustrated and angry with it when it doesn't work properly, to share things with others, and to engage with anyone and everyone. To connect.

L: Yes, but someone built that computer and put those things on there.

G: We understand this, and we are simply using it as a metaphor for the All That Is.

L: I know. I am just playing devil's advocate here because I am a journalist after all. It's my job to question everything.

G: Of course. We know this, but for your readers it is important to clarify.

L: I do understand your reference and metaphor, though, and it does resonate with me.

G: Very good then. You are not one thing. You are all things. The All of Everything. The All of the All. The All That Is. This is you and me and we.

L: Can two people share the same soul on earth? Could I be someone else who is here now living a completely different life in a different place but both of us be alive at the same time?

G: No. For this is not possible upon your planet, Earth; though, it is possible upon other places and planes. You are, however, perfectly capable of being in two places at one time, as we have inscribed here earlier with you, as a human being and as a soul being something other than human. As one sleeps, one wakes. As one wakes, one sleeps.

L: What about twin souls or twin flames?

G: Twin souls are those individuals who feel as if they have been guided to a particular human being because they have been with him or her in other places and upon other planes. Like attracts like, and though it feels as if they are a soul partner, they are in fact a soul attractor. They attracted one another through their thoughts, words, and actions. Their beliefs in the concept of twin souls bind them to one another. Perhaps, though, the notion of twin souls and twin flames has been taken in from another realm, but no, this is truly not possible upon the current planetary evolution of earthly beings. It is possible in other realms, as we have stated here.

L: So there are no other *Lauras* walking around planet Earth right now?

G: Right now, no. In earlier incarnations (in the time-space continuum of earth), certainly yes; you have been here prior many, many times, indeed.

L: Do we keep our personality with us in all incarnations or when we return back to spirit? I consider myself to be funny, kind, loving, smart, sarcastic, silly, and things like that. Have I always been that way, or will I be that way always?

G: This is the nature of evolution. These are the things you take with you along the way. You carry them with you like a calling card—I am kind. I am loving. I am peaceful. I am the sum of all parts. As I grow and evolve, I take with me any and all things that create who I wish to be.

L: So yes?

G: Yes. You take with you into each lifetime the newness you have grown and evolved in other lifetimes' experiences. All the things you have become are who you are as you incarnate into each body form.

L: But if all things are happening all at once, how can that be possible?

G: All things exist as possibility depending upon all thoughts, words, and actions. Whatever possibility has been tapped into in each and every incarnation based on these is how you will grow and evolve into the next. Be smart, and you will be smart in the next. Be brave in this lifetime, and you will be brave in the next. Choose fear in this lifetime, and you may no longer be brave in your next. Does this make sense? Resonate within your soul?

L: Not necessarily.

G: Why?

L: Because I don't think I can quite comprehend the idea of living simultaneous lives and having each life affect the other. If they are all happening simultaneously at different time periods or in different planes and places, how can they have an effect on one another?

G: Because you are being guided to seek inner wisdom throughout each lifetime, and those who do are capable of tapping into their life-driving themes. Once life themes have been dismissed, they dissipate within each incarnation making a particular incarnation easier upon the whole or collective.

L: In our last book you told me I had 772 lifetimes.

G: In this particular universe, yes.

L: Can that number be changed depending on what happens when I get to the end of this lifetime even though they are all happening all at once? See, this is where I get confused. How can all lives be happening at the same time, yet I have lived so many and others not as many?

G: As we have explained in our last book together, there is no time and space in the kingdom of heaven, and therefore, you are able to live as many lives as you possibly could want as individual souls. As a collective soul we are all living just one life, truly, as we are all one. So all of your lives are my lives. I have lived an infinite number of lifetimes because I have split myself into infinite bodies and forms. You have lived a multitude of lifetimes because you have split yourself into a multitude of lifetimes. Think of it the way a cell divides. It all starts from the source cell, which splits itself into infinite parts. Those cells are then capable of splitting themselves into infinite parts, and then those cells are capable of the same. Do you understand now? All the cells came from the same source, and if they were placed back together (no matter how many times they split), they would still be part of the original source. I am experiencing myself through the split cells, which are all part of me as well.

L: I would imagine this is why our bodies work the way they do through cell division.

G: Precisely! Ding. Ding. Ding. Ding. The body works in much the same way. You have different parts of the body, but they are all part of the same whole. All parts affect the whole, and they work in tandem. Makes perfect sense to you now, does it?

L: I think so. I am in shock at how I just came up with that in ten seconds.

G: We came up with that. We write together, never separately. We are writing this as one giant cell. Though you have been split apart into separate cells, whenever one binds back to the original cell, why, then you are capable of the miraculous feat of writing alongside the Oneness. We are all one. Everything I know, you know. Everything you know, we know. Ask me something you don't think you know about. Go on. We know.

L: All righty. What happened to the guy the other day who seemed fascinated by my book but then disappeared on me with no explanation.

G: He went away just as you knew he would.

L: I didn't know he would disappear. Not consciously anyway. And why not just be honest with me that he didn't like or agree with the concepts in the book?

G: Thy truth will set you free or set you up for a conversation you are not interested in having. For not all who come to you will be capable of connecting to this material. They may enjoy it. They may find it interesting, but they also may find it irrational, weird, or crazy. One's ego determines the path here. It is upon you to always remember this when sharing our material with the masses. Though you know it to be true, most, if not all, will find it "blindly" (not knowing they have been unconsciously guided to do so) and, therefore, will not understand its core message, just as you were not able to in the beginning stages of our dialogue. Though you accept it as truth now, there will be many, if not all, who are incapable of understanding its core message until they are truly ready to let go of their own theologies about who and what God really is.

L: Was this perhaps yet another circumstance we could discuss and uncover in these books?

G: Yes, and though we understand you may find some of these circumstances difficult, they are purposeful and, therefore, meant to create powerful conversations from which to grow and evolve.

L: I feel as though you are also saying that most people who read these books are not going to believe me or them.

G: Did anyone believe what was written in *A Course in Miracles* at first?

L: No. I would imagine probably not.

G: No. They did not. They found it all to be quite blasphemous and very nonsensical. They attacked it repeatedly, and yet thirty-five and some odd years later (in human time-space), more and more of your fellow brethren are finding it, reading it, and understanding its core message, the same message we are teaching here—we are all one. We are never separated from that source, and we are always in cocreation whenever we are reminded back to the Oneness.

L: I really want to help people. I really do. When I hear this,

though, I just get hung up on whether or not anyone will want my help.

G: You will find that those who are willing will find you. You have no need to find them, for they will come to you in their willingness whenever they are ready. This is the crux of your illusionary problem from which you are suffering currently: a relentless need to make those who are unwilling understand our collective truth. In their own time frame is when they will come.

L: What is the best way to go about sharing this material and the message, then?

G: Be my messenger. That is all. Share it openly and willingly with whoever comes seeking enlightenment. Get out of your own way so we may make that way for you and through you. Get out of your own way—truer words have not been spoken to you since we started.

"Ask not what can I do for myself; ask what can God and all of the Universe can do for and with me today. I am one with the All That Is. Amen."

L: What can God and all of the Universe do for and with me today?

G: We will guide you from this place of knowing. We will walk you through this if you will let us. Let your conscience be your guide. Whatever conscious thoughts you have in the process, follow them—these are your inspired thoughts. Go with them. Go toward them. Use them. If you see something, say something, do something, or be something. Ask for guidance always when something doesn't align or make sense to you.

"How may I interpret this?" is all you need to say, and an

answer will be revealed unto you—a yes or a no, a smile or a smirk, a nod or a wink. Take it in. Take it all in. You must know we are with you always. Every thought is God thought; all you have to know is that God is always with you, and let no thoughts of ego be allowed in.

I stopped writing, and when I got in my car, the song "You Are Loved (Don't Give Up)" by Josh Groban was playing on my iTunes music. I had not listened to that song in forever, and when I had left my car, my phone had been on an audio book. My phone also normally opens iTunes to the first song in my playlist alphabetically. I knew this song was for me, especially when the next few songs related to being guided by someone else; and the last song before I got to my son's school was "Angel Band," a song my brother introduced me to right before he died.

L: That was a very powerful message for me today through those songs.

G: We know. We felt your gratitude, appreciation, and knowing in that moment of connection.

L: Yet you also then know that as soon as I got home, I was overcome with fear, doubt, and worry.

G: Yes, we know and feel this as well.

L: I am sad that more people won't find this material and won't be changed by it.

G: Are you changed by it?

L: Yes. Completely. But if I am being honest, it's lonely here being in the know when most others are not.

G: We know.

L: I feel all alone in a world where no one wants to hear about spiritual truths or philosophies. They would rather read about sexual harassment and politics or celebrities and gossip. As happy and unburdened as I feel, I also am frustrated, which I would imagine is why I'm struggling.

I closed my eyes for a minute to meditate.

L: I just heard, "Come be with us here." What does that mean?

G: It means do not dwell upon the illusions. Come and sit awhile, and be with us. Close your eyes and return to the Oneness. We will take from you all of your frustrations and upsets. We will guide you back to love so that you may not feel all alone. For you are never alone in the loving arms of the Universe.

I tried to go to that place and meditate but found myself unable to shake the panic and tailspin I was in until in the middle of the night I received a message from Spirit with the phrase, "Go beyond who you think you are, and get to who you truly are." I woke up and immediately wrote it down. Later that day, while at the mall, I walked right past a T-shirt with the phrase, "Go Beyond. Anything is Possible."

L: Yet another powerful message for me. Thank you. I guess

it's hard to ignore these types of signs. As you say, there are no coincidences.

G: And yet you do deny them, don't you sometimes?

L: I do. Not always. Many times, I leap with joy when I see them, but then after a while I forget about them and go back to being frustrated. Because at the end of the day, I am still a human living in a body dealing with the everyday realities that you tell me are illusions. I do understand this concept, and I do absolutely believe in the "we are all one" notion, and, though it makes perfect sense to me, I also don't see the proof yet of the things for which I am asking from a physical standpoint. Money is still not flowing to me the way I would like it to, and so I am having a hard time with the belief that we can draw things to us and always have helpers around us with this.

G: At what point today did you stop and pray for a minute to remove irrational thoughts?

L: Here and there.

G: Here and there is not enough. Here and there is never going to move you forward in the game of life. Here and there will keep you stuck in a pattern of self-justification for not practicing with your spiritual tools because you are not seeing what it is you wish to see.

L: I still don't believe. I don't believe if I put the money out that it will come back to me. I truly cannot get past this particular issue. I get there, and then I slide backward.

I trust, and then I question. What am I doing wrong here? What can we do as humans to move ourselves past this all-encompassing fear of not having enough? I know this whole money issue is purposeful for me to feel this way so that I can understand what others will go through as they begin their spiritual practice, but I am so sick and tired of holding on to this fear. I want to release it forever. I want to move past this issue. I want to have faith.

G: "Have a Little Faith in Me." I sent this song to you one day, and as you walked down the sidewalk, you knew this was for you. You are picturing it now in your mind's eye. Let us put something else in your mind's eye; tell us exactly what you see. You may close your eyes if you would like.

I closed my eyes and saw nothing. My email chimed, and I went to check that.

G: Distractions abound. This is one of your life-driving problems. You are consistently and persistently plagued by distractions. Emails, texts, phone calls. You are a procrastinator of the highest level. To focus one's attention is the greatest gift to anyone seeking higher spiritual truths. Remove the distractions, release the attention to details, and replace the thoughts instantaneously, and miraculous manifestations occur.

L: We are a society attached to our smart phones. It's not just me obviously.

G: We would call them "not so smart phones" because that is what they do, make you all not so smart. These devices of mental incompetence are so prevalent among your society they have replaced connection in every way, shape, and form. No longer do you commune with lovers and friends. Instead you lie around all day typing into a device. A device that seeks to separate you even further than you already are. You place more importance on your everyday musings of chaos than practicing spirituality and then wonder why the manifestations do not occur. Stop doing. Start being. What you are doing is being distracted by anything other than this book or our teachings. Sit down and shut up.

L: Sit down and shut up. Well, that seems pretty harsh!

G: Harsh words do not equal upset. Harsh word equal truth thrown at you in a way that cannot be ignored. You are too busy doing and not being. Though your focus has been on getting this material out to the masses, you have missed the entire point of these books altogether in that is there is nothing you need do, you only need be.

L: Well, perhaps this is where I am getting hung up. How can you be something you say you want to be without doing something about it? Don't we have to take some action toward our desires? You can't just expect something to happen if you sit around watching TV or checking social media all day and don't actually do anything to move toward what it is you desire.

G: "Anti-social media" would be more accurate of a term here. What it is you desire is what I desire for you as well. Don't you see that your will is my will, and therefore, all desires are manifesting?

L: No, I don't see that at all. I see the signs and messages letting me know that we have helpers all around us. I don't, however, see the physical manifestations in front of my face.

G: We know that you know this is not true, because you do have some money coming in. It may not be a lot, but it is enough to move you along the path without going hungry. We know that you have financial stability currently. Though you have financial insecurity in your seemingly real (but very much unreal) illusion-based world, you are not starving, nor are you in danger of going under. You simply are at a standstill, and this is what is burdening you as of yet.

L: Yes. That is all accurate. What is your point?

G: Our point is that under no circumstances are you going to starve, ever. Our point is that you have all you need currently to thrive and survive from a standpoint of being capable of just being.

L: Well, perhaps you see it that way, but I certainly don't. I haven't not worked in some capacity in thirty years. I have always had a paycheck except for a couple of years when I was married and took time off to raise my son. This is the first time where I have no paycheck and no job on the horizon. I am terrified.

G: Good. Now we are getting to the heart of the matter. You have no idea what it means to struggle unt—

L: Until now. Oh my gosh! That is true. I have never had to struggle.

I feel tears welling up in my eyes, and I have goosebumps.

L: My whole life I have always had enough. My parents took care of me, and then I went to work at age fourteen babysitting. This was followed by retail jobs, work as a fitness instructor, and then finally work in television. I have always had money coming in. This is the first time in my life where I feel what it feels like to struggle, to have no idea from where my next paycheck is coming or when it will come. I had a feeling all of this was purposeful for this book. I spent twenty-four hours in a pity party for myself, and yet I knew there was a deeper conversation happening here.

G: We will not steer you wrong. We are with you always and forever.

L: So now that I know what it feels like to struggle, I can guide those who come to me for help, whereas before all of this, I could not relate or comprehend what their fears felt like?

G: Exactly. For this is what all experiences of agitation are all about from here on out. In order to know yourself as the All That Is, you must know all experiences yourself. You have suffered through grief, depression, loss, anger, resentments, bitterness, aging, agitation, emptiness, loneliness, and jealously (among other emotions), but you have never truly known the feeling of struggle. Now you do. And so you can guide others who are in this same position. I see you. I am you. This is your greatest gift for connection. This is how you go from student to teacher. We have said to you so many times that we are with you always, and though you feel this every day, you have denied our existence to strangers and other enlightenment seekers for fear of being judged. This is purposeful as well. You must know what it feels like to have fears of harsh criticism in order to understand how to live life unburdened. To not give a care, as you all would say.

L: Well, we would probably put it less delicately using a four-letter word, but I understand your point.

G: We knew you would.

L: So all of these pent up feelings have been purposeful and brought upon me by—

G: Your soul. Your soul knows what is best for you and will give you exactly what you want whether you want it or not.

L: What do you mean by that?

G: For sometimes you are not wanting things you actually do want, though you do not know that you want them.

L: I feel as if I am on an episode of *Lost* right now. I'm lost.

G: A great show, indeed. What we are meaning to say is that God is not here to tell you what to do; God is here to show you who to be. For this is the soul's only true goal in this life and other lifetimes you are in currently. To do this, sometimes the soul must take you down a darker path and then bring you to the light.

L: I thought that was all ego's doing.

G: Not always is ego in charge. In most cases, if not all, ego has a hold on your thoughts and words but never your actions. Actions are born strictly from the soul. So when an ego thought says, "Go right," when you should have gone left, soul knows best which direction to go and, therefore, will give you exactly what you want—which is to go left, not right. Soul will stop you in your tracks, so to speak. However, in a case such as today's distractions of emails and phone calls, soul knows that you need to take some of these and see some of them so that we may create purposefully the evening's conversation, which you also intuitively knew you were meant to have. Soul always knows what is best for you and will guide you there from a space of knowing what you want and don't want.

L: You still need to explain further the want and don't want aspect. Why would our souls move us toward what we don't want? For instance, I don't want to feel this way about money anymore.

G: Neither do we, but what we do want is for you to inscribe how this all works for others so they may read it here and be reminded of who and what they really are, a soul being a human, not a human being a soul. So in your not wanting to feel fears over money, you are also wanting (from the soul's perspective) to help others lead an unburdened life. Therefore, in your intentions to help others, you are being guided through thoughts, words, and actions to what you do want—which is to help people. One cannot guide others if they have no recollection of feelings they have not had ever or not had in a while. In this way, the soul will guide you toward what you want—though in a way that makes you feel as if you are getting what you don't want. Do you understand any better?

L: Perhaps. But I think I will have to read it a few times to make sure. I find that many times when we are writing this

book that as I am writing something, it makes zero sense to me, but after I read it back several times, it makes perfect sense. Then I feel like a complete dummy because it didn't make sense the first time. Make sense?

G: To us, yes. To your readers probably not. Suffice it to say that anyone who undertakes the reading or listening of this material should seek inner truths whenever a meaning is in question. In this way, there will be no question over what is in question. Ask for clarification whenever you are in a state of confusion from this or any other materials of a spiritual nature.

L: Can you clarify the statement about ego not being involved in an action. What if someone decides to steal or murder? Wouldn't that be a strictly fear-based action to inflict harm? So your statement that ego isn't in charge in most actions, that soul is, doesn't seem to make sense to me here.

G: "No action" is soul's greatest gift to you. Reaction is ego's trick. Soul will guide you toward truth via quiet contemplation. Ego will guide you into past mistakes whenever possible. When action has been attempted, soul will move you toward what you both want and don't want as we have created with you above. When reaction is attempted, ego has the reins.

L: Then the best action is no action?

G: "No action" is getting clear on intention through quietness and contemplation. Moving toward a goal through inspired notions is action at its finest. Most actions in your world view are in fact reactions, and this is where you all are mainly living currently, in reactions.

L: My reaction and aggravation today were for sure born from reaction and living in past mistakes. Was there anything I could have done to get myself out of the funk I was in more quickly?"

G: Yes, but intuitively you knew that you were meant to be in this funk, and so you stayed there purposefully.

L: That is true. I told a friend today that I decided to throw myself a pity party even though I knew exactly what I needed to do to get myself out of it. I just refused to do it and decided instead to go to bed early last night. And, of course, miraculously I had that new mantra come to me in my sleep, "Go beyond who you *think* you are, and get to who you *truly* are."

G: And who are you, truly?

L: A perfect child of the Universe. I am at one with the Creator and all of life. Amen.

G: Amen. Perfection. Absolute perfection.

L: Thank you for all of this and for these powerful conversations. Though I don't like feeling the way I have been, I understand now why I do. I also realize I need to listen more to my intuition because deep down I knew the truth of why I was feeling the way I did.

G: You are welcome. We are here for you always. Your questions are many and never ending. We wish that you go to bed now, and tomorrow we will discuss the idea of karma, which you have been wanting to discuss.

Karma Chameleon

" **D**ear Universal Oneness, together shall we bind minds and create this material for all who come seeking the riches of word and thought written through the channel of a powerful creator and thought leader. Amen. "

Laura: Is there really such a thing as karma, as was initially taught in Eastern philosophy?

God: Yes. All sentient beings upon planet Earth are under the laws of karma, which state that which is an equal and opposite reaction must be explored.

L: Does this requirement happen within every lifetime?

G: Not necessarily, no. Those beings upon your planet who have taken on a notion of newness (in a current incarnation) have brought upon themselves this law of cause and effect. However, this law is not in effect in any and all soulsocieties, as not all beings find it necessary in other incarnations upon other places and planes. But on earth, yes, you are all under the current laws of karma. In every action there is an equal and opposite reaction. This is one of Newton's laws as well as universal law. Good and bad. Up and down. Near and far. Do bad things, get bad things. Do good things, get good things. Simple, isn't it?

L: I don't understand how karma doesn't exist in all places if it is a universal law or principle. May you explain that please here?

G: We may. It is universal law, but it is not a cosmic law. Therefore, it is not at play in other soulcieties, such as those found upon planets outside the current solar system. Have we not told you how in other universes there are other . . . well, there simply are no words in modern language to explain this. We simply would need to say what happens upon your planet and other places within the stratosphere need not happen everywhere.

L: I believe this. I really do.

G: And it is the truth. Have we not told you of the nature of duality? You are not one thing; you are all things, and therefore, there is an equal and opposite reaction to you as well. You being relative to we.

L: So then there are parallel universes as many have believed?

G: There are parallel universes as well as perpendicular universes. There are places and planes that exist that are vastly different and vastly similar. There are more things in the universe than heaven and earth could ever imagine.

L: Meaning what?

G: There are places and planes that are so beyond the scope of the imagination that they cannot be explained here with primitive languages or understandings. Therefore, we must simply state that unless and until all who return to Source Energy are knowing of these truths, not one person living upon your planet will be able to inscribe it here or in other materials. There simply are no words.

L: So no one who had a near-death experience would even be able to describe these places or planes?

G: Not one being upon your planet, Earth, has come far enough ever and remained in a state of being to unveil these truths.

L: Yet you have said that we are all one. So this would seemingly contradict what you have been telling me. If we are all one, then why can't we unlock these rememberings? You here have said we all know the answers within.

G: Do you currently understand the languages known as French, Italian, Spanish, Russian, or Swahili?

L: No. I do not.

G: Do I currently understand these languages and all the others upon your planet?

L: I would imagine yes.

G: And you would imagine correctly. The language of the

inscriber is the language with which you are most familiar in this particular incarnation. You are, however, perfectly capable of unlocking the mystery using all these other languages at will should you decide you wished to do so. Though you would find this hard to believe, would you not?

L: Absolutely. Yes. I would find that hard to believe since I have never studied any of them (with the exception of some Spanish).

G: Well, we are here to tell you that you are perfectly capable of speaking any and all languages upon your planet, Earth, and all languages within the cosmos as well. We will also say that as the current inscriber, you are under the laws of the cosmos, which state that anyone wishing to know universal principles must be willing to overlook certain discrepancies in how this all works. Yes, it is true that we are all one. It is also true, however, that those in body are under strict guidelines stating they may not know everything unless and until they have returned to Source Energy fully and completely. Once as body they have done this, then and only then may our magnificence become fully realized. This is not to say you cannot know about the laws of the universe and cosmos. It is to say that you cannot know all until you have returned to us. Us being relative to we.

L: So when we die, this will all be revealed to us?

G: Yes.

L: And what about those who have had near-death experiences? They can't bring back through this exact type of information?

G: Of course they can. For many of them have had similar revelations. What is true is that they may not remember completely until they have made a choice to disembody fully. There is rhyme and reason as to why this all happens the way it does. For you (as in you all) as a body have made a choice to not see the duality, to not know everything so that you may remember as you go along. To remember all at once would render this whole universal experiment useless. Why come into body for purposes of growing and evolving the soul if you already know all there is to know? What magic is there in revealing what it is you have already witnessed?

L: I guess I can understand that. So why then even allow us to remember the little bit we do? Why allow us to understand the laws of the universe in the first place?

G: Because it is not necessary to not know who and what you truly are fully in order to discover it.

L: Why not? How is that different?

G: If left to their own devices, humans would destroy one another. For this is what has happened in other incarnations upon your planet before its original, or rather, current inception. An experiment gone awry, so to speak. The species' survival depended upon the thoughts, words, and actions of its inhabitants, and rightly did they destroy one another. For they had no reason not to, and so they did. They had no cause and effect. No up and down, left or right. No near or far. Do you see where I am going with this?

L: They had no karma?

G: Yes! They had no karma. Sir Isaac Newton discovered this idea of cause and effect and the law of gravity. And who do you think inspired those discoveries of science?

L: You?

G: We. We all did. We knew that in order to achieve a state of balance upon your planet, we must put into place the notion of cause and effect, and so the law of karma was born. This is why we say you cannot not know who you are. Those beings upon your planet are incapable of self-destruction without it. It is not like this in other worlds where laws may be of a different structure.

L: So explain how karma works on our planet. You have said that both saints and sinners walk together in the kingdom of heaven, which to me implies there is no punishment for doing bad things. You here have said when we do bad things, it is because we are thinking from a place of fear, and therefore, those bad things are not really happening to us; we just think they are.

G: And this is all true. Yet, as you here have said, it does not feel like this. "It all feels very heartachingly real,"[5] as was stated upon the pages of our last book together. And we know this; and so we must explain that relative to the body's understanding of what is happening to and through it, you are at the effect of your cause upon planet Earth. This does not state a case that what is happening is at all real, only that it feels real within the realm of the physical.

L: So when we are in physical form here on earth, then we are under these laws of cause and effect?

G: Yes. You are at cause and effect.

L: So explain this further please. Give me an example of karma at play using my own life please.

G: You may not like to hear this, and you may erase this if you are at all bothered by it being placed here upon the material.

L: Go ahead.

G: You are stubborn, and therefore, you are pushing against yourself. You are refusing to listen to our advice and, therefore, are struggling to survive spiritually. You are angry and are, therefore, maintaining illnesses, which you need not suffer. You are impatient and are, therefore, making yourself wait.

L: Can you be more specific? Like, take something from my past as an example.

G: You have been unwilling to allow us to think your thoughts with you, and therefore, you have been unable to progress to the next level of achievement here.

L: You are still not giving me an example.

G: We have given you several, for you simply are ignoring their meanings here.

L: I am not ignoring them. I do understand your point, but

I don't think you are explaining it well enough. So perhaps I will ask better questions here.

G: All right. Go ahead.

L: What happens if I called someone a name as a child at school?

G: Then you will be made to feel as bad as the person whom you dishonored.

L: What happens if I made fun of people for allowing their children to sleep with them every night?

G: Then you will create a circumstance in which your own child will have a need to sleep within your bed as well.

L: What happens if I made fun of someone for needing reading glasses to see a menu?

G: Then you will at some point be made to feel as if you need glasses as well, which you are currently wearing now, are you not?

L: Sadly, yes. What happens if someone cheats on you?

G: Then that person will betray another as well.

L: But what about the person who has been cheated upon?

G: It is not necessary for them to repeat the cycle. For they have not caused the harm but are at the effect of the harm. You are not at cause, and therefore, there would be no effect.

L: Would the cheater then be betrayed?

G: Eventually yes, though it may not happen within their current lifetime. Some effects may linger into another lifetime.

L: So it is true that we carry our karma into other incarnations?

G: Yes.

L: Well, that is a heavy burden. How do we release that?

G: Why would you want to?

L: Why wouldn't we want to? Why would we want to carry our karma with us?

G: Because you are here to grow and evolve, and yet again, you are thinking from a space of body. Spirit knows all circumstances have value.

L: Do I have any karma to clear from other lifetimes?

G: Yes.

L: Can you tell me what it is?

G: Yes.

L: Go ahead. I'm waiting.

G: You have been a cheater, as we have mentioned within our

last material. In times where divorce would have been painful financially, emotionally, and spiritually (from a religious standpoint at that point in time), you have strayed. You are, therefore, at the effect of this cause, which is why you found yourself in a position where you yourself were presented with this circumstance.

L: Interesting. Because of something I did in a prior lifetime, I was made to feel this way by someone else in this lifetime?

G: Yes.

L: Well, that sucks. I could have done without that feeling.

G: You could have, but you would have never known what it felt like to be on the receiving end of something painful such as the betrayal of a partner of love and romance.

L: Well, I wouldn't call this guy particularly romantic.

G: Betrayal runs deeps. Though you have forgiven this partner and you seemingly are capable of laughing this off, you are still suffering from the effects of his cause. Are you understanding now how all of this works?

L: I think so, yes. I obviously need to release those hidden feelings. May we please say the proper words here to release this?

G: "Dear Universal Oneness, I cannot know what hidden demons lurk beneath the surface. Please release for me any and all notions of unworthiness as they relate to a partner of love and romance. Allow me to see the effects of the cause that harmed my psyche, and together shall we release this feeling of being betrayed forever. Amen."

L: Now that we are on the topic of karma and cheating, can we discuss one of our current issues running rampant in the news cycle the last couple of months? The issue of sexual harassment. I am not even sure what my question is here. I just feel as though it's been talked about so much that I needed to bring it up here.

G: What is your question? You must ask before we can reveal an answer.

L: OK, what is the nature of the struggle between men and women?

G: It goes back to the issue of karma, which is why we inspired you to bring it up here.

L: How does this relate to karma?

G: Karma is at play in all dynamics of a sexual nature. For those inflicting the wounds upon another are merely at the effect of their cause based upon thoughts, words, and actions in any and all lifetimes upon your planet. This is to say bodies are holding on to relationship woes from any and all earthly encounters, be they sexual or not. How ones relate to others is of dire importance in the realm of the physical. For this is reason number one for incarnating into a body. It is so you may learn, evolve, and remember the feeling of physicality. We embody in order to experience sensations such as love, anger, resentment, annoyance, joy, and pettiness (among other emotions). Emotions are the driving force of the human experience. This is why it is such an important one for your soul growth. For it is here upon planet Earth where you can work out your karma in miraculous ways. You can fight. You can make up. You can wander between partners. You can toy with emotions. You can transfer energy through acts of sexual indulgence. You may not, however, under any circumstances design a life where you have not been at cause for some effects.

L: What do you mean by that last sentence?

G: It is upon the all of you to create circumstances where you may move beyond other lifetimes' effects. This is to say as you speak, so shall you seek. Any and all circumstances from which to grow and evolve one's soul are predicated on issues and concerns from other lives' experiences. This is what we are calling your "contracts and agreements," which has been inscribed by other healers. You may go and look this up for yourself if you wish right now.

L: I have heard that phrase before through the teachings of Dr. Peebles, and when I looked it up, I found that a spiritual teacher named Caroline Myss had done extensive work on the subject of sacred contracts.

G: And we would encourage any and all who are reading this material to go and find these teaching for themselves. You also would benefit from these particular teachings as part of your own spiritual curriculum. And now we may explain how this all relates back to your question of understanding why and how these relationship issues are part of the cycle of karma and the like. Many purposes exist for relationships upon your planet,

Earth. They are meant to teach cause and effect as well as grow and evolve the soul beyond circumstances from other lifetimes. When you are of body, you must understand that relationships are necessary as a mirror of one's own self. You are in a state of being, which serves a soul's true purpose, and this is to move beyond a status quo. This is to say you must move forward in the succession of lifetimes by being better than you were before. So in every circumstance is a means to grow and evolve beyond that circumstance so you may get to the next level of enlightenment.

L: Whoa! This is so good and so, well, enlightening to hear. Earth is where we learn about emotions?

G: Earth is where you learn about cause and effect through emotions.

L: Are there other things we learn about on earth?

G: For they are simply too numerous to name here, but we would say your earthly pursuits are of equal and opposite polarities, always. Remember this as you go about your days: consequences. This is our word for what those of body are meant to feel whenever they have undertaken a notion of separation from their source of being.

L: What are some of those consequences?

G: Sexual repression manifesting itself as physical harm toward others would be one, to return back to your original question here. Causing another to feel pain, as you have felt pain. Breaking a leg in a fall, making a mistake on a test question you would otherwise have known the answer to, presenting an award to a person who you don't feel deserves it. These are consequences you have all experienced based on actions and reactions in circumstances from other incarnations or lifetimes. You are always at the effect of your cause.

L: So we can't escape our karma, but it may not present itself in this lifetime, and we might be at the mercy of karma from other simultaneous lives?

G: Precisely accurate. Yes.

L: Well, I can honestly say I don't really want to experience consequence in this life for things I did or do in other lifetimes; How can I fix this?

G: You can't. There is no need to "fix" this, as you say, only to remind yourself of who and what you truly are so that you may learn these lessons through love and not fear. One cannot escape these karmic lessons. However, one can learn them through the lens of love and not fear thereby making his or her earthly time (of which we are speaking here) more enjoyable.

L: Can we uncover these karmic debts?

G: Yes. Through focused intention and meditation, these are always at your fingertips. Close your eyes; let us release one now with you here so that others may benefit from your teachings.

L: My intention is to learn of some of my karmic debts right now. Dear God, please reveal them to me now.

I closed my eyes and listened.

L: "You have been at cause for the murder of two children," is what I just heard. Seriously?

G: Yes.

L: Oh, gee. Well, that's just great. Thanks a lot for that painful revelation from another lifetime.

G: You need to first ask me about the circumstances.

L: OK, what were the circumstances?

G: You were left by a man who was abusive toward you and your children. You were bound and gagged and left for dead, and therefore, in your fear, you manifested a scenario where they were taken from you and destroyed. Though you did not pull the trigger or cause their demise physically, your fear created a circumstance in which you were tortured, as were they.

L: This is not the story I was expecting to hear. How long ago was this? Did this happen here on earth?

G: Yes, in the late 1500s/early 1600s.

L: And so that was the cause; what was the effect, and how was it carried out in another lifetime?

G: We will ask you to close your eyes again so that we may reveal an answer.

I closed my eyes.

L: I heard, "Nothing yet." So I have not dealt with the consequences of this action? So what would an effect look like for this cause? It doesn't sound as though I was a murderer. More so that I was too afraid to try to save my children.

G: Yes. Your fear has caused what we would term a delayed reaction. You have yet to deal with this horrific, tragic circumstance and pushed it aside to be dealt with at some point in other lifetimes.

L: Why would I do that?

G: There are some circumstances that may be too painful to watch as you seek to grow and evolve, and so you cast them aside to be dealt with at a later time.

L: But why would I not want to deal with it? What would be the consequence for this?

G: That would be for you to decide, and upon this you have not decided.

L: Can I do something to change the circumstance or consequence?

G: Yes.

L: And what would that be?

G: We will reveal it here now. Close your eyes again. Take a deep breath, and wait for the answer to be revealed.

I closed my eyes and took a deep breath.

L: I saw myself reuniting with those two children. They run over to me and give me a giant hug and are so happy to see me. "Mommy!" I hear them yell.

G: This is your consequence. You have been without these dear children century after century. You have been unable to forgive yourself, and so you have willed them away. For you have no need to travel through lifetime after lifetime anymore holding on to this circumstance. You may release the demons within holding you hostage to your deep anguish and despair.

L: Is there a proper prayer here to further release this?

G: "Dear God, for too long I have held on to the notion that I am a bad mother, unworthy and incapable of being a mother to my children whom I have lost in previous incarnations. It was not my choice to lose them, but rather, I was at the effect and cause of a man who suffered from a darkness and depression he could not control. It was not my fault they died, and yet my fear led me astray from the source of all being, and in my fear they perished. I cannot continue to hold on to this despair for one minute longer, and so I ask, dear God, for this contract to be broken for all of eternity. I am a being of light. I am a mother of many, many children. I bring them to me and through me. Amen."

L: This is all really crazy, and actually it's kind of scary because

I can only imagine the kind of deep, dark, subconscious demons we are holding on to from other lifetimes that are holding us back from living joyous lives. I would have never in a million years thought of something like that and obviously would have never known it was affecting my life.

G: This is the reason quiet contemplation is necessary daily, if not hourly. Remind yourself instantaneously of who and what you really are, a spirit being a human. Ask yourself, "Where am I holding on to fear?" on daily repeat so we may reveal these inner truths to you and through you. Then may they be released to the nothing from which they came.

L: I think I sort of get the whole "nothing" concept. You say it this way because those things that come from fear are not really happening to us? They are just manifestations of our fears?

G: Yes. Though there is more to it than human minds can reveal here.

I wound up finding a healing center where I was able to do a meditation into parallel lives. It took me into that lifetime, and I watched myself as a soul trying to speak to this woman and get her up off the floor to go save her children, but ultimately, she couldn't. I watched her die and reunite with her children as spirits.

L: I have to say that experience was profound and restorative for me. I would imagine this is how our soul/spirit speaks to us, but if we don't listen, then our fear takes over and we—

G: Reunite. Remember it is not tragic to die. The *you* who you were witnessing in meditation had no idea of who was speaking from within.

L: So I could not help her even though our souls tried from within.

G: Your soul is doing this with you right now.

L: In this lifetime, I am able to listen, though.

G: Precisely. Listen and know with whom you are speaking.

L: Could I have saved her?

G: No. A healing occurred on both levels, though, and for this we are profoundly grateful.

L: Why?

G: Because you have released a deep subconscious life-driving altercation that may have been affecting this life journey.

L: And I also feel a burden was lifted by my forgiving of the man who did the damage in that lifetime. It felt as though that may have been a struggle I carried with me without knowing as well.

G: Indeed. A very good job. Well done.

L: There are some in the new thought community who believe

we don't carry our karma with us into other lifetimes. Can you clarify this for me?

G: We may. To answer a question such as this you must know all lives are happening simultaneously as we have previously explained here with you. To know you are the sum of all parts is to know you are at cause for the all that happens upon your world both inner and outer. Those beings choosing to evolve through circumstances of an opposite reactionary pattern may very well carry karma through to other lifetimes while those who choose not to, do not. Do you see how both meanings are possible?

L: No.

G: You are the chooser of what to experience.

L: But you stated that we have these contracts and agreements we have to work out from other lifetimes. "You may not, however, under any circumstances design a life where you have not been at cause for some effects." So I am completely confused on this. Why does one healer say we don't have karma follow us into other lives and you are saying we do. If there is only one truth which is it?

G: It is of what you believe which is most important. You believe in karma. She or he may not.

L: But again if there is only one truth of the universe how can this be possible?

G: There is but one truth. We are all one being of light separated into millions upon trillions of parts. You are expressing these truths as part of the Oneness and as individual consciousness. It is of what you believe which is most importance. One healer may interpret karma as a necessary process of a single life. Another may express it as you have done here.

L: Well that makes it seem as if multiple truths exists.

G: The law of cause and effect is truth. How you interpret its use is up to you.

The next day after the meditation about the karmic debt, I felt very depressed for some reason.

L: That hit me like a ton of bricks. Why am I struggling? Shouldn't I be feeling better after a heavy burden has been lifted?

G: All of this is hard work. It is not easy to be a spiritual being when you are in a body (be it human or one of another world). It is because you are in a body that you struggle as you do. The minute you feel an emotion such as anger, resentment, or depression, you forget your spiritual path. Your tool box is right there at the ready, but you refuse to use it. Oh, you try here and there, as you said earlier, but you are still hung up on your problems and not your solution.

L: And what is the solution?

G: Practicing spiritual philosophy day by day, hour by hour, minute by minute until you get to a point where any and all attacks by the ego are rendered harmless.

L: It's so hard to practice minute by minute. It's also hard to get past the stark reality of not seeing the manifestations in your life. So yes, I get caught back up. And if I am being honest, I still struggle daily over whether or not this is all real or made up in my head. Even though I know how these books were created and how I am not capable of writing this well, I still get caught up in the judgement of others. How will others view me? Who will believe me? How can I prove some random journalist is talking to the energy of the Universe or God or Source or whatever you want to call it? I am still embarrassed to admit it because I know most people will think I am completely nuts. I am scared of being harshly judged. I am scared of being alone. I am scared of ruining my finances and my career.

G: Are you done?

L: I think so, yes. I feel sick.

G: You are sick. You are sick and tired of being unable to maintain your spiritual composure here. You have fought long and hard to stay afloat, to stay above the fray. You are, however, winning this battle. Although it does not feel like this to you now, it will. Someday soon you will be in a place of such spiritual knowing that you will look back upon these books and laugh at how silly you were acting here. You are spiritually sound. You have the tools and know the principles. You are capable of teaching and preaching at the highest level. You are simply at the cause of your effect.

L: And what effect is that?

G: Wanting to know beyond a shadow of a doubt how real these conversations have been. You are, therefore, at cause for the unhappy feelings created by these books. Simply put, you have been messing with yourself. You know this. You feel this. You have no need to suffer. You have a need only to thrive. Yet you do not know this, and so you suffer the consequences of irrational thinking so that you may know yourself as irrational. Now you know what it feels like to suffer at the hands of negative thinking.

L: Why must I continue to suffer like this? I feel as though these books have been all about making me struggle and suffer through anguish in order to write these questions. I honestly don't want to feel like this anymore. I want to feel at peace. I want to stop questioning the validity of these books. I want to trust. I want to have faith. I will myself to stop fighting inner demons and start trusting the Universe explicitly.

"Dear God, as we seek to share these books with our readers, may we remind them of who and what they truly are, spiritual beings inside of bodies, bodies needing constant attention. Bodies needing focused intentions and powerful prayers to function perfectly. Minds needing to be watered and fed spiritual knowledge. Remind me, remind we of our connection to the All That Is so that we may create whole perfect bodies and lives. Amen."

You wrote that, didn't you?

G: We wrote that. We are always in cocreation here now. You know all of this is very purposeful. You have to get through all the ways things can go wrong before you can teach how to make it right.

L: I know it, but I don't like it. I don't want to do this anymore. I don't want to struggle anymore. I sound like a broken record, and I hate it.

G: There will always be circumstances to overcome. As a teacher, it will be upon you to remind those seeking enlightenment that there are no perfect days. There are perfect moments, perfect hours, and perfect windows of time but not perfect days. Within each and every miraculous day of life upon your planet (and others) is a way to grow and evolve through all sorts of circumstances. This is the nature of your being human (and otherworldly creations), and it, therefore, is upon you to know this so that we may guide you throughout your days through better circumstances using the tool of love and not fear. It truly is as simple as this. Each and every time you think a thought that underserves your true nature, you activate the switch that keeps those lights on. We have stated this as a matter of fact in our first book to you. Think yourself anew. One cannot underestimate the force of power that is your thought processes whereby all manifestations arise. You are not your thoughts. Your thoughts are you. You are the master in charge. You are the general commanding the troops. Do not allow the ego to do this for you, for it will bring you results you do not like. You are the caretaker of your life, no one else. We will walk you through this if you will let us. We will guide you through the demons and bring you to the other side of knowing. You are a miraculous, unstoppable being of light and love. The only thing stopping you is you. You make the way. You are the way and the light. I am the flashlight, and you are the tunnel. Everything you want is on the other side of fear.

L: It doesn't seem after writing this book that we can easily get to the other side of fear. It sounds as though most of us, if not all, have some inner demons to work through subconsciously. So in order to thrive and survive as spiritual beings, we have to uncover and unlock these.

G: There is no hard-and-fast rule on this, but yes, much of what you carry, you carry from other lifetimes' circumstances. It is always best, therefore, when in quiet contemplation to cocreate with the voice within the answers to any and all past, present, or future lifetimes' circumstances.

"Where am I holding on to fear?" we have told you before is a most important question in releasing inner demons.

Doing this daily will make a marked improvement in your lifetimes. Circumstances needn't arise as often nor be as difficult once all demons have been revealed and released.

L: Can you walk me through some of my current ailments.

G: Current illusionary ailments. Yes. Fire away. We are ready to reveal an answer to your current illusion-based woes.

L: My heels. Every time I struggle with the knowing, my heels hurt, making it hard to walk.

G: I walk in the light of knowing that I am far from enough. Therefore, I bare down on my heel in pain.

L: And how may I release this?

G: "Dear God, Father Almighty, Being of light, please take from me any and all notions of separation as they relate to my need to control everything. I walk in the light of knowing I am enough. I am."

L: My skin is on fire right now.

G: I rage underneath my skin. Everything is bothering me right now. Everything is getting under my skin.

L: And how may I release this?

G: "I marvel at the beauty I see in the mirror. I walk in the light of knowing I am safe and guided in the loving arms of the Universe. I am truly at one with the All That Is."

L: I cannot get rid of this belly fat no matter how much I exercise or how well I eat. This is a problem most women face for some reason.

G: "I carry with me the wounds of my past mistakes. I hold on to them inside where my gut instinct is located, a safe space to hide my anguish."

L: And how may we release this?

G: "I am guided by an unseen force who releases with me the heavy burdens I carry so that I may feel spiritually full."

L: I'm going to work on that one for sure. It's certainly an interesting way to look at our gut health issues. I will say my dreams have been so much more vivid these days. As I write these books, I feel as if they become more valid in showing me spiritual truth, hidden fears, or other lifetimes' circumstances.

G: All of the above are true.

L: The other night I had a dream about a lion eating a panda

bear, or trying to anyway. May we please accurately interpret this powerful dream's message?

G: We may. A lion consuming a bear is a metaphor for the unnerving feeling you have about releasing these books and materials, specifically your first one. By the time you release our second book, all fears, doubts, and worries will have been alleviated. You shall note for your readers how the irrational-minded nature of your thinking was perpetuated by your soul's desire to manifest for you the feeling of anger, resentment, and bitterness toward yourself in order to move you toward your life's goal of being a healer. One (of a healing profession) cannot be that which they say they wish to be unless they have been shown the way through the dark. In order to grow and evolve as a speaker, healer, and teacher of spiritual principles, you must have known what it feels like to be at one with the ego.

L: And why would our soul make us do that? Or more specifically, why would my soul want me to be made to feel that way?

G: You are enlightened beyond a shadow of a doubt now. You are casting aside all previous notions of who and what God and the Universe are or are all about. Are you here now to walk in faith and seek guidance within from your spiritual cheerleaders, your cocreators, for all of eternity?

L: I am. Thank you.

G: You are very welcome. We are here for you always in every circumstance, of which you will have many, as all of you are here to grow and evolve in circumstances of equal and opposite polarity.

L: Speaking of circumstances, thank you for helping me today at the doctor's office. I had to have that atypical mole removed by a surgeon, and it was actually quite easy and painless. I walked in with no fear and allowed the Universe (and my dad and brother) to come with me metaphysically.

G: A circumstance in which you were made to feel as if you were at cause for the visage.

L: I heard you say this earlier, "At cause for the visage." Can you explain what that meant please here?

G: You are at cause for the way you feel about yourself whenever you look upon yourself in the mirror. To view yourself as perfect and beautiful always will cause you to see a perfect being staring back at you. To look at yourself as old, tired, or ugly will cause you to manifest certain diseases within the body. Because you have had a friend diagnosed with and subsequently "die" of a skin disease called melanoma, you have taken within your psyche the notion that you may be able to have this happen to you as well. Therefore, this is why you have manifested, not once but twice, a circumstance surrounding your skin, which caused you to seek medical attention and surgery. You have no need for these fear-based medical modalities. However, unless and until you clear all blocks to salvation, you may very well be at cause for this again and again. It is upon you, then, to create a circumstance in which any and all attacks against the self are eradicated through focused modalities of prayer and intention.

L: Well, my intention is to see a whole, perfect body and face from here on out. My intention is to no longer create a situation where I am at cause for anymore skin cancer, lesions,

or moles. What would be a proper prayer to repeat to release the inner demons?

G: "Dear God Almighty, Keeper of truth, show me the evidence of my whole and perfect body. For I am a beautiful creation of all of the Universe. I have no need to suffer inside a body. For I allow the soul to shine through, radiant and glowing. I release the need to feed my unworthiness through outside pursuits. Instead, I turn inward and state, 'I am a child of all of the Universe. I am worthy. I am whole. I am perfect exactly as I am, always and forever.' I share this message eternally with all who I have been before and all I will be after. For we are one with each other, and together we are all perfect and whole. Amen."

L: Yet you have said there will always be circumstances to deal with in those bodies. I mean, at some point we, well, our bodies anyway, are going to die, so there has to be a little bit of suffering, right?

G: Not necessarily. You are forgetting that all of the all of you are at cause for the thoughts you think. You are perfectly capable of leaving the earthly plane in a calm, quiet, and painless manner. Go to sleep, and good night. This is the death sentence most would enjoy, and all of the all are capable of this ending sensation if this is what they so choose. If a soul chooses a different path for itself, then it will know pain and suffering but only as a means to grow and evolve. To know this truth, you must be consistent in your daily practice of quietude and contemplation so you will know this has been a chosen circumstance, and then you may learn through love and be guided home lovingly and with a loving hand outstretched to and through you.

L: Can we ever come back into a body (incarnate) and live a joyous, unburdened life here on earth from start to finish?

G: No. Circumstances always will arise from which to grow and evolve. You can, however, live a purposefully joyful life if you are purposefully creating your life this way by using the tools and techniques we have prescribed for you and inscribed with you here and with other healers and masters. Your lows will be mostly highs, and this is why we teach here with you: so that others may understand spiritual wisdom and seek to release the enslavement of ego-based thinking.

God Can't Fix the Toilet

"*Dear God as we seek to inform other beings, let us now remind them through focused intention how to design a life of grandeur. Amen.*"

Laura: Today was a good day. While I was looking at new houses for my mom, this man was out walking his dog, and when he looked over at me, he looked just like my dad. It made my heart leap with joy to know my dad was with us yet again. It's hard not being with him physically, but having those profound moments is so incredibly helpful.

God: We are glad you are enjoying our ways of connecting. These vivid moments are available to all whenever thoughts align. Our worlds collide.

L: I would love if it could be more often.

G: It can if you will ask. The more often you ask, the more often it will happen. We are with you always. In all ways. There is no one we are not. There is no one you are not. So you may connect with your crossed loved ones over and over again in moment after moment. As long as you are asking, we are obliging. Our ways of connecting are vastly different from your human ways. Still, we are with you metaphysically in any and all circumstances. "Yours for the taking," is how we will say all of you can commune with those you have lost in human body form.

L: Thank you. Well, I love those magic moments. Part of what I want to be able to do is allow others to experience these miracles too. I want to help those who are grieving understand their connection to the All That Is.

G: And you will. Oh, my dear child, you will. You will lead those seeking shelter to their truths.

L: I understand that when we incarnate, we separate ourselves but can return to the knowing we are that Oneness in any instant. What about when we die and return to spirit form? In heaven are we always all one, or can we also be separate?

G: In spirit form you are one while being separate as well. We are all one always, but we are also capable of separating from the Oneness for purposes of growing and evolving our souls. You are capable of creating yourself anew to inscribe how all of this works. You are fully capable as well of being both creator and created so that you may do that. So you are the writer (a separate individual), and you are the listener (the spirit), and you are the author (a.k.a. God). Body-mind-soul.

L: I fully get that. I don't think it answers the question of what

happens when we die, though. Are there individual spirits in heaven? We don't have bodies there, correct?

G: One can if they want to, though most do not choose this, as it can be very cumbersome. You can embody if you want, but more so you choose to stay in spirit form, as it's much more manageable a state of being. We do, however, embody for purposes of greeting our loved ones who have crossed until said time as they are understanding of the connection to the All That Is.

L: So we are individuals as spirits too?

G: Yes. You are all things all at once. You are spirit incarnated as body. You are embodied as Laura the individual soul. However, you are also a soul in heaven with me here now.

L: As an individual?

G: Yes and you are part of me as well.

L: I'm confused.

G: We know. For you are waiting for the perfect answer of how this all works so that you may control the outcome. However, this is not how we have designed the system for you all as bodies. You must be "kept in the dark" in some aspects as a means to grow and evolve. This does not mean at some point all may understand perfectly the concept of being both everything and nothing at all, but it simply is not feasible to reveal all of life's great mysteries. We would if we could, but we can't, so we won't.

L: Why can't you?

G: So you may know yourself as the body you are in currently. You cannot know fully what it is to be human if you know fully what it is to be spirit. Whenever you return to the kingdom (through mindful meditation and prayer), may you remember more and more pieces of the puzzle. Until that time, keep practicing and preaching, and more will become available to you, to all of you. Wherever you are at, be grateful to that place.

L: Will we ever know all as individual bodies and souls here on earth?

G: No. As we had inscribed here prior, there are simply not enough words in your primitive languages to describe in vivid detail all circumstances from which you may grow and evolve. This does not mean you should not try. For all who go seeking inner truths will unlock a mystery of epic proportions. There are a few who walk among you who do know all, and this is quite purposeful, as they are helpers here to help you evolve and remember. They, however, are knowing who they are already and have, therefore, decided to incarnate for very specific purposes.

L: Am I one of these people?

G: No. You are knowing you are not, just as they know they are. You must understand there are many layers of creation, and though you fight to remember them, you know you are not meant to, so you don't. Make sense?

L: I guess. So some things about the way this all works are kept hidden from us, by us purposefully.

G: So you may know yourself experientially as the All That Is. You are of this world (meaning spirit or heaven) but not in this world, and until you are, much of what is really going on here will be undiscoverable, and this is done purposefully by you and for you.

L: I have a question about soul mates and contracts and agreements. It sounded to me as if we are meant to meet a certain person and have a certain experience as part of our evolvement process, and we set contracts for this. But in our first book you said there are no such thing as soul mates.

G: That we did. As it relates to partnerships of love and romance.

L: So can you explain that? If during our contracts we have agreed to meet a specific partner or person, then would that person not be a "soul mate" to us in a sense when we stumbled upon them at some point in our earthly journeys?

G: "Soul mates" is not an accurate term here to describe these agreed-upon arrangements. For simply have you made a gentleman's (or gentlewoman's) agreement to work upon each other's soul contracts together. A "soul mate" is a human term made by man to define someone as a perfect partner of love and romance. There are a million perfect partners you may encounter. For whenever you have made the choice to incarnate, you are always capable of incorporating a love partnership into your life. You are not, however, at the whim of your contracts and agreements here. Therefore, a soul mate is a chosen circumstance by you and for you while in a body. We are all perfect partners to one another in heaven, and so there is no reason to define something like this as a spirit. Are you understanding here?

L: Yes. What about if one of our agreements may be forgiveness, and the partner we choose winds up being someone we need to forgive? Was this perhaps something set in advance?

G: Perhaps. But remember you always will have free will. So this is why it is wrong to say something or someone was "meant to be." For you always will have choice in the matter. Even if you have decided on the idea (as spirit) to comingle with another soul, it is always possible that you may never meet or come across this person as a body. This is why we would not deem anyone or anything "meant to be," as you simply have many, many choices in all circumstances based on the actions of love or fear.

L: I think that explains it well enough. Thank you.

G: You are welcome. As always, we are grateful for this time spent in cocreation. May we wish you a very happy new day as well.

L: Don't you mean new year?

G: New day. New year. It does not matter. It is all the same. Only as bodies is when a calendar is necessary. We have no need for timekeeping here within the kingdom.

L: Can you tell me about my meditation this morning. I am trying to make more time to meditate. I have a hard time quieting my mind and settling down, but this morning I was able to do it. I had a meditation that showed me being swallowed by a lion in a gladiator-style arena. May you please explain its meaning to me?

G: We shall. May we remind you in quiet contemplation is where all good thoughts lie.

L: That did not seem like a very good thought. It seemed as if a lion made me its snack.

G: It did. Yes. But it also made you its victim. And this is your metaphor. Right now, you are feeling as if you are a victim of your circumstances. "Let no one harm my psyche other than me." This is the wisdom of the lion. Never shall you be a victim of outside circumstances. Always shall you be reminded of your inner nature, a soul being a human. I am at the will of my thoughts. I am my thoughts. I create what I see. I feel what I create. I do what an ego wants.

L: How best can we get out of doing what our ego wants though?

G: Ego wants to distract and disarm you so its agenda may be fulfilled. Think of your ego as if it's a little child, selfish, spoiled and whiny. This is an ego mind distracted by its surroundings.

L: As I read back through this book with you to remove anything that is inaccurate or stemming from an ego mind, I am reminded that we have revealed some radical ideas about health and illnesses. I want to make it clear to those reading this book that we are not saying here to not go see a doctor for a proper diagnosis. We are simply reminding people of their spiritual natures and capabilities of mindfulness and meditative modalities. I myself have been at cause for my skin cancer diagnosis and my reoccurring psoriasis issue and other ailments, such as infertility and hair loss. Each and every

one of us has some deep spiritual cleansing to deal with, and releasing these inner subconscious-level thoughts can take time and be difficult. While it is my intent to heal and not harm anyone, I want to make sure we are clear that we are in no way here telling people not to seek medical advice or attention.

G: As we have said many times here, you are not impervious to illness and, therefore, must always seek medical attention whenever (and as) irrational thoughts persist. This is not to say our modalities of unlearning all you thought you knew are not remedies for an ailment. We are merely reminding everyone that unless and until all notices of separation are healed both subconsciously and consciously, a medical opinion is not only practical and preferable but absolutely a must for all enlightenment seekers.

L: Had I not caught my skin cancer diagnosis early enough, who knows what could have happened?

G: Listen to your gut instinct. This is a truth and always reliable.

L: I should have listened to my gut instinct about the mole on my face and have it removed sooner. I knew something wasn't right with it.

G: And you are bound by this knowingness.

L: I would like to put my knowingness on my finances.

G: And so let's do that here.

L: All right. I am ready; hit me with it.

G: "Dear God and All of the Universe, I am knowing that I am a creator of the created, and never again shall I live in a notion of poverty or lack. I am a powerful magnet of money and all things that I deem important to my life as a being being human. Amen."

L: I enjoy all these elaborate prayers, but are they truly necessary?

G: They are tools, powerful tools, indeed, but not necessary in terms of being the only thing or only way to obtain that which you are wanting or needing, desiring, or proclaiming. Beings capable of understanding their connection to the All That Is need only remember their connection to the All That Is, and rightly they may obtain that upon which they place their awareness. Prayer is a simple tool or practice for obtainment, and that is why we teach it here and with other spiritual messengers or guardians.

L: That makes perfect sense. So it's more a teaching tool than an absolute necessity once you are confident in your knowing?

G: Precisely. We would warn you, though, to continue using it as the teaching device it is meant to be, as all who come seeking this re-information may be unready to understand our oneness.

L: I will do that, then. Thank you. I am grateful as always for our wisdom. You can't just let me write "me" or "I" can you. There is always a "we" or "our" component.

G: You are we, and we are you. You are also in control, as you always have free will, but we enjoy your ego being cast aside so we may join with you in choir. For you are a powerful channel (as all of you are capable of becoming).

L: You are in my head now more and more. I wake up from sleeping with powerful words and phrases being right at the top of my mind. I have these crazy, vivid, amazing dreams, and that's if I even can sleep. I want to just write and write and write. Just when I think we are done, I have question after question after question. Donald Trump as of today is still in office as our current president. Today he described several countries as "shithole countries" that are predominantly populated by races other than his favorite, which is white people. Half the country was enraged; the other half was engaged—as in cheering him on. We are so divided as a nation. I don't even know what my question is here. You mentioned in our last book that all of this crazy weather and these natural disasters we were having were in direct correlation to the fears permeating our nation. Yesterday there were some very serious and tragic mudslides in California and last month parts of Southern California were engulfed in flames. I have to ask again if all these weather-related incidents are still stemming from the collective anger we are all feeling in our country right now.

G: They are, indeed.

L: So you are still claiming climate change is not at play here.

G: We are simply stating a truth that the collective consciousness is at cause for all weather-related issues, be the issues caused by fear as it relates to your current president or fear as it relates to how you all are treating planet Earth. You are all at cause for the all of everything as we have said.

L: Then it is a little bit of both?

G: It is both the collective and individual consciousness that are at cause, yes.

L: So God does not punish us as some believe with these tragedies.

G: God does not punish. Period. Consequences are brought about by the laws of cause and effect, be those consequences weather or something else tragic or triumphant.

L: But the people who died, I just don't think it's fair to cast a massive burden like that.

G: It is both fair and accurate to say they are at cause. For we cannot know the prevalent thoughts that brought about the circumstance. One only need understand in relation to the All That Is that all get what it is they desire for their souls' growth. Look upon these tragedies for that which they are, which is circumstances from which to grow and evolve the soul. This is the design of the universe, and that is the *soul* purpose of misfortune.

L: So you are saying yet again that these people's souls knew or planned the path, and this is why they died.

G: Yes. This is why all "die" or cross over and leave the body behind. Once they leave, they are understanding of that soul decision.

L: Leaving their families behind to pick up the pieces of their shattered lives. Great system you have designed here, buddy.

G: Again you are thinking from a space of body whereby you cannot understand or comprehend our unlearning modalities through which there are no shortages of ways to grow and evolve. Soul knows all, and when you are back in the loving arms of the Universe, you will understand fully and completely your purpose upon earth and other planes and places.

L: It's hard to look at a story in the news where a child was killed or died tragically and not be upset at this system that was designed to grow and evolve our souls. When it comes to children, our hearts are just too weak to understand the whys of loss here. It breaks my heart to think of anyone losing a child, whether it's illusion or not.

G: Our children. These are our children as well. Know that they are safe, guided, and loved by the Universe as well, and nothing happens without their first having been a thought about it, be it spirit, soul, or ego driven.

L: Still doesn't make me feel any better.

G: We know, but we will tell you how to make it easier upon your psyche.

"Dear God and All of the Universe, as it relates to children, know that our collective's consciousness is wiser than we know, and therefore, is understanding of the laws of cause and effect as they relate to any and all beings upon planet Earth. Let no one suffer a fate that has not happened through them and to them. Allow all manifestations of fear to be wiped away and love to shine through on all my fellow beings of light. Amen."

L: Not helping. I still don't see the need for children getting sick, being injured, or dying. I say this from a place of love.

G: Is it love, or is it fear?

L: It feels like love to me. Children are sweet and innocent and bring mainly joy to our lives. Why is it necessary for them to suffer?

G: It is not necessary for anyone to suffer inside bodies. It is, however, necessary to grow and evolve through circumstances of opposite polarities, and it is, therefore, a necessary portion of humanity.

L: I understand it, but I don't like it.

G: We know. However, the design of the universe is such that our collective beingness manifests itself upon an entire world, be it liked or not. As we all have said before, God does not pick whom to harm and whom to heal. Only is this found within the collective thought systems at play in all worlds simultaneously.

Today is Tuesday, January 16, 2018. My first book, **The All of Everything**, *has just been released.*

G: You have been busy.

L: We know. And we are back to the "we." You love to make me write "we" instead of "I."

G: We enjoy the argument you have within yourself over what

to keep and what to erase. We are two books in, and still you are doubting what is actually happening here.

L: Only because people look at me funny when I tell them about these books. It's hard to explain to some people, especially those who are not in the enlightened community.

G: There are not many people, no. A sliver of a percentage of the people upon your planet, Earth.

L: And most people don't believe any of this. They live in the illusion. I mean, sure people buy into meditation, and some are convinced there are angels helping us while others believe our loved ones who have crossed over can communicate with us, but most people are not convinced that anything we have written in this book (or our last one) is truth.

G: Do you believe what has been written here?

L: I do.

G: All of it?

L: Most of it, if not all. Some concepts are a little out there. So I can understand some of the people's trepidation, but it seems most people don't even believe in 10 percent of it.

G: Something is better than nothing.

L: True.

G: You must let those who are willing come to their own

conclusions. It is not upon you to wake anyone up other than yourself.

L: So why did we write these books?

G: So that the truth is revealed through someone with a skeptic's eye. This does not mean, however, you are in charge of the waking. You are simply in charge of the sharing of said material. That is all you need do. Share it willingly with whoever comes along willingly. For in your knowing will you allow their knowing to begin.

L: So simply hold space for them so that they may arrive there on their own.

G: Precisely. Without judgement. Hold space without judgement.

L: Yes, I am struggling with that part. I don't know if I would call it judgement or something else. I sat today in a room full of people in various stages of learning and unlearning and found myself frustrated at how many people are still asleep. I feel called to help them, but I guess I am still figuring out the best way to help people.

G: Be an example, not a scolder.

L: What do you mean by that?

G: You shall not scold someone for not being right where you are. Rather, it is upon all beings of light to hold space for other beings of light so that they too may find their own paths toward salvation.

It's hard being a human. Being a soul is easy. If you could only learn to harness the inner being more, why, then what a magical life you would all live.

L: But we can't just sit idly and wait for something to happen. We need to take an action don't we?

G: An action, yes. A reaction, no; and this is what you are doing. You are reacting to systems that are within your control. You control the shape of things, and what we mean to say by this is that forever are you in control of your destiny through the creative power of your thoughts. You are in the driver's seat here, and yet you still have not kept the windows down and let the breeze flow through your hair. You are bound by the ego mind striving for success and adulation. What you do not yet understand is you only need to be.

L: Maybe I just don't understand what that means. What does it mean to just be?

G: Be quiet. Be still. Be open to guidance. Be present and aware of your surroundings.

L: But again, I would say you can't just sit around meditating all day and expect the perfect job or the right relationship to land in your lap. You have to do something to move the ball forward, don't you?

G: If I told you you didn't, would you believe me?

L: Nope. Not at all.

G: And thus your main issue has been revealed. You do not

believe that your cocaptains along for the ride will guide the journey. And so for this reason, then, yes, you must take actions.

L: So you are telling me if I just sat around all day meditating and being still and aware, I could manifest the life of my dreams?

G: Yes. What you believe, you can achieve (though it would be difficult, if not nearly impossible, for the all of the all of you to do such a thing because you are in various stages of learning and unlearning, and so yes, as it currently stands you must take some actions toward your dreams). This does not mean that you have to spend every waking moment in intense mode. For has this not been the crux of your current illusional problem of manifesting perceived illnesses for yourself?

L: Yes. I have been going full throttle with book promotion, and my skin is on fire. I went on a sugar detox to see if that would fix the skin, and it hasn't helped at all. I can feel the stress my body is under. I have been doing, doing, doing, and my body is suffering because of it.

G: Diss-ease. This is why you suffer.

L: As in I am dissing the ease? Meaning I am fighting against things being easy. So when I heard yesterday in my mind, "Less doing. More being," this was a message for me.

G: Without a doubt, which is how the all of you should live your lives—without a doubt.

L: So the skin issues tie back into my need to do and my lack

of faith and trust. What about my current clogged toilet in my house that I am dealing with today?

G: Clogged thinking will always manifest itself in some extravagant way as a means to show you what is happening within one's mind, reminding you that nothing happens to you that does not happen through you.

L: So every circumstance that arises in our lives is meant to shine a light upon our mindset and what we are creating at that given moment?

G: Yes. No exceptions. This is a universal fact. All circumstances upon your planet, Earth, lend opportunities to enlighten and heal.

L: And how would we get rid of these types of everyday pesky life issues?

G: "Dear God, I cannot understand the reason behind this current mess I am in. May you please interpret this accurately for me so that we may heal the hurt, as this is what was at cause. Show me the thought process that led the circumstance to be presented to me, through me. Amen."

L: Great. I will do that. Dear God, I cannot understand the reason behind this current mess I am in. May you please interpret this accurately for me so that we may heal the hurt, as this is what was at cause. Show me the thought process that led the circumstance to be presented to me, through me. Amen.

G: "I am not a teacher of spiritual philosophy, and therefore, I must prove my worthiness to others through outside means."

L: And how can I unclog my thinking?

G: "I am a perfect child of all of the Universe, and together we bring about change for our planet. I have no need to do, only to be. And so I relinquish the need to be as intensely proactive as I once had been. I know all roads have been paved and all asks have been answered, and so I wait patiently, silently for my dreams to begin to take hold. Amen."

I tried to fix the clogged toilet myself using tips and techniques I found on YouTube. I also prayed about the issue and set intentions, but nothing worked. Finally, I had to call a plumber.

L: Well, I prayed, I set intentions, and I asked for help, and my toilet actually is still not working properly. In fact, I think I might have made it worse. So I guess God can't fix the toilet?

G: God can absolutely fix the toilet, but when you are so focused on the problem, you can't get to the solution.

L: I turned it over to God and the Universe for transformation, and my mess still persists.

G: What you resist persists. Why not just call a plumber in the first place?

L: Because toilet clogs (and I can't believe we are even talking

about this in a book that will one day be read by millions of people) are an everyday occurrence and sometimes easy to fix.

G: So are eating, sleeping, going to the bathroom, waking up, and enjoying a sandwich.

L: What is your point here?

G: Our point is that focusing upon the problem will bring about more of the problem. Focus upon the solution.

L: And what was the solution?

G: Call a plumber.

L: Seriously? I'm sorry, but I just disagree here. It renders all this spiritual mumbo jumbo kind of moot here if the answer is calling a plumber rather than calling upon our higher selves, inner voices, holy spirit, God etc.

G: God can't fix the toilet, as in God can't physically use its energetic hands (which you all have because we are all just one great being of love and light) but can send you a perfect person to help solve the problem. Focusing upon the problem creates more of the problem. This is universal spiritual law. May we ask why you did not take the practical step first?

L: Because plumbers cost money and can often times overcharge and scam you for things you don't need.

G: Said the collective consciousness. OK, go on.

L: And as I said before, I gave it to God to transform my illusional problem.

G: "Call a plumber." We had offered this message to you in words spoken through you, but you ignored it in favor of ego's tricks— go online and try to fix it yourself.

L: But why call a plumber? Why can't God fix the toilet?

G: Because God is not a plumber but rather a facilitator who will send you who and what you need when you need it. Perhaps an intention set surrounding the issue may have been better, something like, "My intention is to cure this illusional problem I am having quickly and efficiently with the right person coming at the right time to fix it who charges me a fair and accurate price."

Not every solution will be the one you are expecting. Sometimes the fix will be one you are avoiding. And why may we ask were you avoiding the plumber?

L: The money aspect of it.

G: Fear. Money is a fear magnet. You have all you need. Lose the fear, and money will arrive in abundance.

L: Does this apply as well to doctors? If we have medical issues, should we also not be waiting around and praying/ setting intentions, etc.? Should we also get medical advice?

G: Always. Always seek medical advice first. For this is why we have doctors here in the first place. Unless and until all irrational thoughts are replaced and wiped away, all sentient beings upon your planet, Earth, are at cause for the many ailments within your bodily structure. Seek attention as well as seek inner guidance simultaneously. This is the best way to defeat bodily invaders, such as your skin problems and current illusional illnesses. You are one who avoids a doctor at all costs, literally. Pay now, or pay later. It is much better to have peace of mind at the same time as having peace of pocketbook. All monies have and will be provided through you and to you as long as you are in alignment with our core beliefs—you are at one with all of the Universe. You have no need to ask, only to receive. "I receive this money with joyous applause. Thank you for my abundance."

L: Back to the clogged thinking. I feel as though I am living on a lonely island. There are so many people living within the illusion; I am not sure at this point how to be a soul being a human when most people are in a state of unawareness. I don't know how to connect with people, because I both see and feel how they are living their lives unconsciously. There is a lot of sadness within me about this. What can I do to help myself out of these dark fears and feelings I am having about being one of only a few in my life who understand our connection to the Universe? My body is a disease disaster right now. I am under so much stress I—

G: Have hope. You do have hope, do you not?

L: Yes. I have hope.

G: Then you have all you need. You must *be* a little more and *do* a little less. We do not say to stop what you are doing. Baby steps are needed in order to learn how to walk. Eventually, a child figures it all out on its own, but it has to at least take the baby steps first.

L: I do have hope but I will admit I am still struggling with this whole aging thing. When you made your living on television, it's hard to watch as you grow older and less and less useful to a world obsessed with beauty and youth.

G: As always, you are at the mercy of all of the thoughts surrounding you. The collective consciousness is obsessed with youth and beauty. This does not mean, however, that you cannot break free of this cycle. In your knowing are you set free, if and only if, you are understanding of this cycle or pattern you are in. Breaking the cycle can be difficult which is why we are here with you always. It may take years to remove deeply embedded insecurities which persist and insist inside one's thinking mind that they are not good enough to be seen, to be heard, to be taken seriously.

L: Well, what can I do? How can I view myself differently? I don't feel as if it's something I am capable of doing on my own. I have tried and still come back to the same feelings and thoughts. I replace them. They return. I still judge people based on what they look like instead of who they are, which is what most of society does as well.

G: And you would be absolutely correct in this. There is a way to break free from the collective consciousness as we have stated here. "I am wholly perfect and beautiful. I walk among my dear brethren and declare they are as well. I see beauty and light wherever I go. I focus upon the light colors around them rather than the body surrounding them. Amen."

L: Is it really possible to do this, to see colors or auras?

G: For this is how we see you. We see the aura surrounding you.

The body is of no importance to us whatsoever. It's simply a tool for learning, not a presentation of who and what you truly are.

L: But as humans, are we capable of such a feat, of seeing each other as our auras?

G: Of course you may do this, though most of you do not know how. And so you focus upon the body. To focus upon an aura, one must cast aside all previous notions of who they were and see who they are.

L: I looked at myself, and I didn't see an aura, but I did hear the words "violet purple."

G: You are clairaudient, which means your hearing sense is stronger than your vision sense. This is how you may "see" auras. Others upon your planet, Earth, may hear auras as well. Some may see them. Others may both see and hear them.

L: So do we each have unique spiritual gifts we are better in tune with (which is why some of us are clairvoyant and others clairsentient and so on)?

G: You are all both everything and nothing at all times. Within each particular incarnation, a chosen gift may be expressed through you, which would explain further your sense of hearing.

L: So what does a violet/purple aura represent?

G: Truth and honor.

L: What about a yellow aura?

G: Faith without trust.

L: A red aura?

G: Loneliness and sadness.

L: A blue aura?

G: Strength and commitment.

L: A green aura?

G: Honor and self-righteousness.

L: Is this how you know what we are working upon and where we are in our spiritual journey?

G: Yes. This is also how we know who is communing from a sense of true commitment and understanding to spiritual growth.

L: Can your aura change over time?

G: Absolutely. It can and does all of the time. When you are feeling low, your vibrational energy will match the color. So when you are weak and tired you may vibrate a dull yellow tinge. When you are exuberant and feeling on top of the world, your color will match this as well.

L: What is the color system?

G: ROYGBIV and everything in between, which is why variances of color occur to some who are visually inclined healers upon planet Earth.

L: The rainbow. Red, orange, yellow, green, blue, indigo, violet. What does the orange aura represent?

G: On a journey to healing. A very long one, indeed.

L: What does the indigo aura stand for?

G: Energy and strength. It is the aura of children mostly. Children can withstand so much because they are an energy level (especially when they are younger) so close to Love.

L: That does make sense. Is this where the term Indigo child originated?

G: Yes. For all children are Indigo children until they begin to understand their connection to the human condition. It is in the condition where they have been transferred or reduced, and their auras will begin to glow based upon their thoughts, words, and actions.

I took another break from writing for a week or two to promote my first book.

G: It's been a while since you have joined us here.

L: I know, and I apologize. I have been busy.

G: We know. Too busy we might add.

L: I knew you were going to say that.

G: You are busy yet again doing and forgetting your beingness.

L: I know. How do we get to the beingness and to core beliefs? I do believe in this concept of cocreation and having cheerleaders along the way. What I don't believe is that manifestations can arise instantaneously, because for the most part that is not how it has worked for me. Instants are more like weeks or months. Nothing is happening overnight. I guess this is where my frustration lies.

G: All frustrations are born of wrong-minded thinking, and this is why you wait. Deny the truth, and the truth awaits your acceptance. Affirm the truth, and the truth reveals itself almost immediately. I am a perfect child of all of the Universe and am capable of being that which I say I wish to be.

L: I don't deny the truth. I deny that it can happen instantaneously. I understand the concept that we can be anything we say we wish to be. What happens is that I get hung up on the time frame. If it's not happening now, it must not be happening for me. I can't seem to delineate the difference between my thoughts being the reason something isn't occurring in my life or if my soul is keeping it from me purposefully as a tool to grow and evolve. You said in our last book, "Nothing happens to you that does not happen through you,"[6] and this baffles me. So as an example if my book isn't selling, then it's my fault you are saying? Or does my soul not want me to sell books right now to teach me a lesson? How can it be both, or can it be both?

G: Absolutely it can be both. It is both. Nothing happens to you that does not happen through you. Let's break this down into a few parts.

First, nothing happens to you that is not through you. From a soul perspective, this means that you are at the will of your soul, which wants for you what it is you want for you. So if you are wanting to be a famous author, you will be. However, if you are wanting to be a famous author but also are wanting material for purposes of creating another book, your soul will give you more waiting so that we may discuss this here.

Second, nothing is happening to you that is not through you as both individual and collective consciousness. So you are at the mercy of the thoughts of the collective, which means, for example, if you were living upon planet Earth and an earthquake shook the ground, then you would be, as part of the collective, caught up in that circumstance. This is not to say you may not be unscathed or unharmed in the presence of unenlightened souls, but rather, you cannot escape the collective's need for a shift in presentation of the earth's core. So you are caught up in the collective mind's shift as well.

L: I understand that. But what about the individual conscious portion of that?

G: You are always responsible for the collective and individual thoughts systems, which all upon your planet have implanted within them. As individuals, all thoughts are your responsibility.

L: Well, explain to me in the case of a woman who was raped or attacked. You are telling me this is her fault and that she was at cause for this?

G: Yes, insomuch as she is caught up in the illusion of separation and is, therefore, at cause for a circumstance that is tragic on a humanistic level but divine from a soul perspective, as it is part of her journey to healing separation from any and all lifetimes.

L: So this would be part three of this explanation?

G: Of course. There are always three parts to everything (as we have explained how this is the natural course of the universe). A trifecta of wills, if you will.

The third part is that all souls are at cause for recognition of self. Recog—this is to say all who come to know themselves as the Oneness are knowing of which goals they have yet to attain in each and every circumstance and each and every lifetime. So if one has yet to comprehend what it feels like to be violated, then one may never know what it feels like to be free of sexual burdens and repressions.

L: I find this hard to believe.

G: Why?

L: Because why would anyone, any soul, purposefully put himself or herself through a tragic circumstance, such as abuse of any kind, be it sexual or not?

G: To experience polarity, yin and yang, up and down, left and right. Divinity comes in many forms, and for this we are understanding of your fear-based reaction to these spiritual truths, but you must understand them in order to grow and evolve as a soul. You cannot know one thing without knowing the other. There simply is no other way to experience all there is to experience.

L: So how do people who are in a body form move past this from a humanistic standpoint?

G: Know that for all intents and purposes, said circumstance is nothing but a truthful presentation of spiritual laws and principles and that should they turn back to the Creator and know they too are the Creator, they can move past it and onto greener pastures more quickly. A true spiritual warrior knows that which is both true and untrue.

L: Yes, but someone caught up in a circumstance like that is surely not someone who is on a journey to enlightenment yet as a body.

G: It would not be necessary to indulge in spiritual pursuits to understand the true nature of the spirit. One's inner guidance systems know the truth for them, and should they use this mechanism, healing is always upon and within them.

L: Is there a way to break through to the soul and ease the frustration of waiting for manifestations to arise at their time frames?

G: No. For soul always knows what is best. So if you are wanting to move past a certain issue, it would be best to understand this and allow the soul to work through you. Working together is the best way to ensure creation manifests quickly and efficiently.

"My dear, dear soul, I cannot know what is best for you; only you do. So I hand over the reins to you so that we may control the flow together as one. Amen."

L: Well, this goes back to the idea of being abused or assaulted.

Why would a soul believe this is what's best for itself if the All That Is is all knowing, all loving? Surely that is not what is best for anyone.

G: In the eyes of the law it is.

L: What law?

G: Universal law. And you know this is what would be said here, but you wait for us to say it for you. This is how soul and knowing work. You know the answer within and refuse to reveal it here yourself. The answer you refuse to speak is that no action in the eyes of the universal law is ever unloving, because, as we have told you here repeatedly, only love is real, and so a circumstance such as rape or abortion or abuse of any kind does not exist in the eyes of the All That Is.

L: I just can't find a way to explain this to a person who doesn't understand or believe in spiritual principles. I just can't explain it away this way because in physical body form, it feels heartachingly real, and I will say this over and over again, perhaps forever, as we write these books and material.

G: You might, or you might not. For there will come a point when you may be able to understand this notion for yourself.

L: It's not that I can't understand it. However, I have been emotionally abused. I have been physically assaulted and I have been through grief and depression. The pain is a real sensation. My skin issues and other ailments feel real. The metallic taste in my mouth feels very real right now.

G: You are fighting off a cold.

L: I figured that might be the case.

G: And it is, and you are easily capable of releasing it to the Universe.

L: Dear God, please take from me the inner subconscious thoughts surrounding my current mouth problem so that I may wake up healthy in the morning. Amen.

G: Very good.

L: Sure I said that, but what happens if my soul decides it's best for me to have a cold?

G: Then you will get a cold.

L: Ugh. So then what is the use for prayers and affirmations? It would seem that they are useless if we can't break through the soul's desires and the ego's as well. I feel as though in human bodies we are pretty much screwed here. Why even bother doing anything if we have no say in the matter?

G: You have all say in a matter.

L: Well, it certainly does not seem like that. It seems as if we have zero say and are just little puppets or pawns in the game of souls.

G: This is not true. We are simply saying that in order to create the life you desire, you must understand the laws of our universe and cosmos, which allow for all circumstances to be experienced, then examined, and then transformed. What if I told you a girl who had been victimized in this life was victimized as a means to move her toward a life's goal of healing others. Would you believe me?

L: Of course. That makes sense, but why can't she become a healer without being a—

G: Victim of circumstance? This is not how the cycle works. In order to know anything, you must also know its complete opposite. You must be up in order to be down. Right in order to be left. You can't be one without the other. A true healer is born whenever a trauma is birthed. This is not to say she may not have become a healer through some other mechanism. Remember, all are at cause for the experience they most need to have as a soul, and whenever you are of body, you are at cause for whether you learn this through love or fear.

L: Well, give me a scenario of how she may have learned through love and not fear and become a healer of some sort.

G: In order to grow and evolve as a soul, she must have some circumstances in her life. This could have involved an angry mother or an abusive father. It could have been a crude and inappropriate boss or an angry mob attacking her values and ideals.

L: How would that be learning through love?

G: Love comes in many forms. An angry mother does not equal a mother who does not love her child deeply. An angry father and verbally punishing boss are simply transferring their attitudes of the world they see around them onto others. This does not mean that person is unloving. This is why we say you must see through the visage and body and into the soul. There you will see who that person truly is and past the outward personalities they project into the world. You are a kind and decent woman who tries to see the best in all people. Though you would admit this can often be a struggle.

L: Sometimes, yes.

G: Imagine what it feels like for those who are uninformed in the ways of love and light to see beyond the body into the soul. For this is why so much anger exists within your planetary system.

L: Yet again I find myself at a loss for words. I am just not sure what to say to that.

G: Trust the soul. For this is our lesson here for you tonight and why you took to your computer at this precise timing.

L: Speaking of bosses, what about work. Often times we are hung up on the time delay as it relates to our career aspirations. Is the soul giving us what we want by someone not returning our phone call or email?

G: One need not spend as much time pursuing success as they should spend pursuing inner attainment of peace and serenity.

L: As I said before, you cannot just sit around and meditate in a cabin and the roof caves in with millions of dollars for you. You have to do something though, right?

G: Do something. Do nothing. It does not matter. It matters

who you are being not who you are trying to be. If you could see that which you say you wish to be within the mind's eye then you are there. However, most are incapable of such a feat and so yes, then we would say in order to manifest a hearts true desires you must take some actions towards your intentions. Some action, not reactions.

"I can't do this. I can't be this. This person will not see me in a new light."

These are reactions not action. Action steps are those which move you towards life goals from a space of pure intention – "I am going to be a thought leader. I am sending this as a means to connect and not as a means to share information. I am auditioning for the sheer joy of the chase not the joy of the win. I am being proactive and not reactive. I enjoy doing the things I am doing to promote my book."

One must never do anything out of obligation, only out of inspiration. When you choose out of obligation, you are often times at odds with a soul's desires. When you move out of inspiration, you are always at cause for its reaction to occur. Share with love, and love returns. Share with anger, and anger or emptiness occurs.

L: So this is why my emails don't get returned. Our intentions are not pure; they are clouded with a little bit of anger, annoyance, or frustration.

G: Yes. A miraculous presentation we might add. Love is a magnet. Money is a magnet. Children are magnets. Weather is a magnet. Nothing returns to you without pure intention.

L: So when we start to view "work" from a space of joy, we will begin to manifest a better result for ourselves?

G: Precisely. Beyond all reason and doubt is truth, and this is your truth. Share with joy, and joy returns. Share with doubt and fear, and doubt and fear return. A mirror held up to anything will reveal itself back to itself.

L: That's a very profound statement. Before we move on, I have a question I forgot to ask about a dream of mine. I woke up one morning and very clearly heard a voice say, "Go buy a lottery ticket." I followed that inner voice and bought one but wound up not winning anything. So what was the point of that?

G: Be mindful of ego's tricks. For when you are awake and asleep, our ego is along for the ride. Simply put, when you are experiencing a circumstance such as you had described here, you must turn to the Universal Presence and ask, "Is this ego or is this truth?"

L: Easy enough. Thank you.

G: Yet most will ignore it here, and forever will truth be lost.

L: Well, I understand it, and so I am grateful for the advice, and I will start to ask for clarification on my dream state and my waking state. This is my goal and intention for the new year: to live my life consciously. We are toward the end of this book, and I am finding myself turning more and more to the higher self, Universal Oneness. I use affirmations. I pray. I ask for help. I meditate the best I can, and yet I do still struggle a little. How do I get to the peaceful portion of my life? Where am I holding on to fear? Please show me now.

G: Your fears are one and the same. Each stems from the same illusion—separation. You believe the answer is outside of you.

L: Of course I do. You have been telling me for two books now to turn to God within, the Holy Spirit within, and my irrational fears will be healed instantaneously. Now you are saying I don't need you?

G: You don't need us, because you are us. You are the source as much as everyone is the source. A good rule of thumb is to turn to God within, the Holy Spirit, as a means to find salvation. Is it the only way? Of course not. It is the way of most enlightenment seekers because it will allow them to arrive faster at the destination. We share it with you here as a means to help others on their journeys. For not all may understand universal concepts unless they stumble upon it at a basic level. Absolute divine truth is this—you are the God within. What you do for one, you do for all. What you say to all, you say to you. What you give to yourself, you give to all. I am.

L: Are you saying that I am capable of healing myself, of helping myself, and of praying to myself through myself?

G: To the divine soul, you are. It is necessary for those first coming to universal principles to use prayer and intention as if it's something outside of them. This will help them along their journeys to know a powerful presence exists, which guides them on their journeys. The only difference we speak with you here now is this—you are that source.

L: I don't think I quite understand what you are saying here.

G: You are the Divine One. All of you. Each of you. It lives inside of you. You need only use the Divine Mind to bring to you whatever it is you desire. The power lies within you. It is you. You are creator just as you are receiver. There is nothing you need do. It is necessary you only be. To be means to understand the power lives within you. So in order to be it, just see it.

L: So how do we tap into this beingness? How do we cocreate with the Divine Mind that dwells inside of us?

G: Be at peace with who and what you are—the creator of the Creator who creates alongside all others. Live with this knowledge and knowing, and let all thoughts be guided by this principle. We are one mind. One love. One giant being of magnificence that lives in you, that is you. Life itself. This is who you are.

L: So then if I am the Divine Soul and I help myself, what do I say when fear strikes within my thoughts?

G: You say, "Dear God, All Powerful Being of light who lives inside of me, let us forsake all fear-minded irrational thoughts and remove them from the Divine Mind. For I know that I am this mind, and I am the creator of the Creator. I choose and accept the following in my life." And then state whatever you wish Divine Mind to create for you—a new job, a new love, a new car, a light fixture, a whole, healthy body. And then await results with a grateful heart, and allow and accept this into your life.

L: So is this what I have been doing wrong? Thinking there is a power outside of me?

G: There is a power outside of you, but also there is the power inside of you. They are one and the same.

L: This is what you mean by the separation; I think that only the power outside of me is doing the work rather than knowing the power inside of me is also in charge?

G: Yes.

L: So why, then, did you make me write these books as if I were talking to God when in actuality I was talking to—

G: All of us. You are speaking with and to all of us together.

L: So when we write, I am using both powers—the within and the without.

G: Yes. To use one without the other will bring about a book of inaccuracies. This is why as you write, you pray to be sure that only what is of Divine Mind is presented, and together we may remove any and all ego-created material.

L: Was anything from our first book inaccurate?

G: Not at all. It remains accurate and to this day resonates with those seeking a new voice. We will do the same with this book's material. As we cocreate, we will remove any and all words that are of ego. As your book is released upon earth, it will be true and accurate.

L: What if I use my free will to share it without praying over it?

G: Then some would be accurate and some inaccurate. For this is precisely how the Bible and other biblical materials were created. Some of the passages are perfectly accurate, and some are ego created. To decipher which are which, one may ask oneself within, "Is this accurate?" to know what is truth and what is ego.

L: Why is it so hard to shake the fear, the ego?

G: Perhaps it has been hard for you on purpose.

L: You have said this before.

G: And it is the truth. We know this process has been painful and difficult for you. The reasoning is obvious. It has been your intention to share a message of hope and change, and in that intention have come some struggles. Not all of life will be easy. Some issues will arise, and it is upon all beings of light to understand growth of soul is a pathway to truth. Truth is often hard to reveal whenever you are of body. Soul knows all for you, so to turn to Divine Mind reminds you that you are cocreators, and what's good for the goose is good for the gander.

L: So we should accept life challenges as they come?

G: Always. Accept them. Bless them. Understand their purposes. Learn from them, and then move to a higher choice.

"I am at one with all of the Universe, and I thank you for showing me the way and the light. I accept all choices as my own and learn and grow from them."

L: My question, then, becomes this: how can we release ourselves from the collective consciousness so that we are not creating circumstances caused by its thinking? For example, right now there is a major flu virus going around. Lots of little kids have tragically died, and everyone keeps talking about how bad it is right now. Panic is spreading.

G: Have no fear. This is how you are released from the collective irrationalities.

L: In our first book, you clearly stated that some things as a collective you are bound to—for instance cellular-level aging. You said enlightened healers will not look much younger, because they are tied to the collective consciousness, which believes so much in aging at a cellular level.

G: Cellular-level biology is an intrinsic truth of your people. It cannot be intrinsically changed without a collective swap of ideologies. A circumstance such as influenza is irrational-mind thinking creating from itself a manifestation of disease. Fear created it. Aging is a belief, a concept of creationism manifesting itself as it does in cellular-level breakdown.

L: My last questions are these: How do we move through the disappointment when we don't see the manifestations of our desires happening? How do we calmly weather the storms of waiting and not allow our doubts to continue to trip us up? How do we get to the absolute faith and knowing that despite seeing no evidence anything is going to change, we will be rewarded in the end?

G: All good things come to those who wait. Do you remember waiting for your son to arrive and how dark and scary it seemed at times as the clock ticked by? Do you remember feeling empty and alone, and yet you did find a new love in your life? Do you remember waiting and wishing upon a star for a career of being on television? Do you recall the time you stubbed a toe and waited for it to heal as you struggled through the pain, and it did heal? Remembering is why you suffer. In the remembering of what has happened, you are stuck in the happening. All must live their lives from a space of unknowingness. You must not know what you know in order to grow. Stop letting what has happened in the past ruin the future. Live in the now. Be here now. The only moment you have is now. Know now. This is the best advice we have for you here today. Live in the now, not in the know. Knowing who and what you truly are is how you get to living in the now. Who and what you truly are is the manifestation of Source Energy. All who come to read and relate to these books are already knowing this within. Once they know within, they will begin to see the hard parts begin to transform. It happens not overnight but through studied practice of the principles and laws of the universe:

- There is only one moment ever, and it is right now. Be here now.
- You are at cause for the all of everything. There is nothing you don't create as mind, body, and soul together. The trifecta is the creative spirit within, and together you grow.
- You are not separated from the source of all being ever. It lives within you. It is you. To know yourself as I know myself is a soul's true goal, and this, and only this, will grant inner peace. To know yourself as the Oneness, to see all as I see all, to love all as I love all is your true purpose here on earth and in heaven. To walk among your fellow brethren and declare, "We are all one and the

same," is the power within deciding upon the truth for itself and all others.

- You move the body toward manifestation with the guidance of Spirit, angels, and life itself. Let your conscience be your guide. Give up the struggle by allowing the struggle to be avoided through cocreation. Do nothing alone. Think as one.
- Ego's role in the illusion is to make you feel as if you are alone and interrupt the flow of love. Do not let the ego run the show. Never let the love go; hold on to it, and cherish it, for it is there with you always.

We have enjoyed our time together so much and wish that you go forth and live your life from these principles above. Allow the beauty of who you are at the core to demonstrate to all who come seeking this reinformation who we are. Live the truth, and the truth will set you free.

And so I did. After seven months of writing, I finally started being consistent with my daily spiritual practices. I awoke every morning and stated the following: "Today I give my thoughts back to the Universe. I shall think no thoughts on my own and seek to be guided back to love in any and all circumstances."

I started taking yoga again. I found time to meditate every single day. I released negative thoughts instantaneously as they came up, and I reminded myself of my true nature as much as possible. I also chose to step away more and more from technology devices and social media and spend more time in nature. I chose to be more and do less.

L: I am forever grateful for these books. I have been changed through them. Jobs have come my way. People have reached out to me saying how they have been inspired by my story and book. I've been interviewed several times on television and for

magazines. It feels as though my fears, doubts, and worries that I have been holding onto to create these two books have finally been alleviated. I am feeling more and more at peace every day. Thank you, God/Spirit, for all you have taught me, or more so reminded me of here.

G: The caterpillar has become the butterfly. There will be many more questions to arise within the days and weeks ahead, and we will create a third and final book in this series together. We are here for you always and wish that you go forth without fear and allow us to guide you with and from Love. Amen.

Final Thoughts

As you receive this reinformation, know that I live these truths every day, and my story reflects this. The reality I experience has changed, and I am so grateful for the beautiful signs, messages, and synchronicities that show up in my life.

When I read through the pages of this book, I laugh at the difficulty I had grasping all of these ideas—just as God said I would. I finally see God from a higher perspective: we are all a part of this magic of life, this one energy source, this Divine Mind. We are one. I am God. You are God. We are God.

Don't be discouraged by my lack of understanding and my struggle to follow the words as I wrote. Be encouraged by them. Let my mistakes, my trials, and my tribulations guide you. My skepticism made me the perfect conduit for writing a book like this.

I know now for certain we are here to grow and evolve as humans by working our way through the circumstances. We set up this system together as one. God/Source created us, and then as cocreators we created the world we see together. We share one mind, and when we work together, we are powerful beyond measure. When we separate from Source, we are islands of one fighting to survive. We either learn this or we eventually "die." But if we connect back to the mainland—Source Energy—we can cocreate a way to experience life's magic.

Put your future in the hands of God, Divine Mind—that one energy who knows the way. Don't worry about the word you use for that source, and simply go with whatever word is best for you in the moment. Pray for God to unlock the door to your happiness so that you may step through to a new reality, and allow the Universe to guide your thoughts back to Love. This is who you are. Accept that this source lives within you, and connect back to your divine Spirit as often as possible.

We all have to deal with life's ups and downs. My prayer is that reading my journey helps get you to enlightenment just a little faster than I did. Remember, though, that the work—the consistent practice of your spiritual tools—is up to you.

ACKNOWLEDGMENTS

God, the Universe, Divine Mind, Spirit, Inner Being—whatever you are called—thank you for being my cocreator on this journey. Because of your guidance, I was able to step out of my comfort zone and show myself love the way we all should.

Megan Langston, thank you for keeping my words true to the messages I received while making sure they weren't full of typos. It's hard to type as fast as Spirit communicates.

Wendy Kis, thank you for transforming the design ideas I had inside my head into the beautiful cover you created.

Melinda Martin, thank you for making the process of releasing a book simple and easy. Without you holding my hand again, I may not have made it.

Mike, thank you for allowing our relationship to flourish after Jason died and for believing in me when so many others did not.

Brenner and Mom, my most heartfelt thanks go to you for always being my biggest cheerleaders here on earth alongside Dad and Jason, the best metaphysical ones in heaven.

Endnotes

1   Walsch, Neale Donald. *Conversations with God, an Uncommon Dialogue.* Hampton Roads Pub., 1997.

2   Hicks, Esther and Jerry Hicks. The Law of Attraction: The Basics of the Teachings of Abraham. Createspace Independent Pub, 2012

3   "The Oprah Winfrey Show." Harpo Productions. 2004

4   Saltman, Laura. *The All of Everything, A Spiritual Guide to Inner World Domination.* Savaah Media., 2018.

5   Saltman, Laura. *The All of Everything, A Spiritual Guide to Inner World Domination.* Savaah Media., 2018.

6   Saltman, Laura. *The All of Everything, A Spiritual Guide to Inner World Domination.* Savaah Media., 2018.

Made in the USA
Lexington, KY
28 September 2018